Unleashing God's Mystery Power

"Christ in you, the hope of glory"

It's all about Jesus

Helen Wiley

God's Mystery Servant

Cover Photo: Romolo Tavani/shutterstock.com

Scripture quotations used in this book are taken from the
Holy Bible, New International Version (NIV).
Copyright © 1973, 1978, 1984 International Bible Society.
Used by permission of Zondervan Bible Publishers
under Gratis Use Guidelines.
All rights reserved worldwide. www.zondervan.com

Copyright © 2017 God's Mystery Servant

All rights reserved.

Printed by CreateSpace, an Amazon.com Company

ISBN-13: 978-1976387050

ISBN-10: 1976387051

Unleashing God's Mystery Power
Table of Contents

Preface	4
Introduction	6
Part One – The Person of God's Mystery Power	9
Chapter 1 – Reading Jesus	10
Chapter 2 – The Path to Life	15
Chapter 3 – God's Mystery Story	21
Part Two – The Greatness of God's Mystery Power	29
Chapter 4 – Crucifixion Power	30
Chapter 5 – Resurrection Power	39
Chapter 6 – Exaltation Power	47
Part Three – The Path to God's Mystery Power	57
Chapter 7 – Faith Works	58
Chapter 8 – Grace Liberates	66
Chapter 9 – Spirit Energizes	73
Part Four – The Delights of God's Mystery Power	83
Chapter 10 – Making Love with Jesus	84
Chapter 11 – Finding Real Success	94
Chapter 12 – Showing off Jesus	102
Chapter 13 – Taught by God	108
Chapter 14 – Finding Real Life	115
Conclusion – Life in the Eye of the Needle	122

Preface

Ever since my teenage years, I believed that there is so much more than the traditional Christianity that I knew growing up. This restlessness of spirit has driven me to bow humbly before the Lord to beg Him to deliver me from all of Satan's cheap counterfeits and to lead me into the reality of what life to the full in Jesus is supposed to be. And I am so overwhelmed with all that the Lord has done in my life to answer that prayer.

I am still very much on the journey. I have not arrived. I am sharing from the perspective of what the Lord has taught me up to this point of time in my life. And I anticipate that by the time you are reading these thoughts, the Lord will have led me to a more complete understanding of His reality. But if I wait until I have everything all figured out, I'll never be able to share anything. So I am simply sharing as a traveler on a journey, in the midst of the discovery.

I also realize that I am writing from the unique perspective of my personal journey with the Lord. We all come from our own unique backgrounds, experiences, failures, disappointments, successes and joys. But I believe that the Lord is leading all of us to the same destination – of a love relationship with Him filled with passion and excitement. So I offer these insights and experiences from my personal spiritual journey in the hope they will encourage you on your own unique journey, as we all press on toward that same goal of knowing and loving God.

I am not interested in producing some polished manuscript that will impress people with my skills and hard work. All I want to do is to share some of the lessons the Lord has been teaching me throughout my life to encourage you to let the Lord work in your life as well. My desire is simply to keep all the focus on Jesus and

His amazing grace at work in our lives, so we will all let Him work in our lives however He desires.

NOTES:

- Scripture quotations are from the New International Version (1984) with some modifications where I preferred my translation from the Greek.
- I crystallized these summaries of what God has been teaching me during 2017.
- Who I am is irrelevant because this is all about Jesus and not me. But for those who are interested, I have been blessed to grow up with godly parents who led me to Jesus early in life, to be married to my wonderful wife Elsie for over 49 years, to enjoy six wonderful children (Mike and Letitia Yoder, Jonathan and Kim Wiley, Cort and Katrina Walker), to have ten wonderful grandchildren (Hannah, Joshua, Cedric, Alecia Yoder; Kate, Jackson, Harrison Wiley; Janelle, Ethan, Isaac Walker), to have some great education at Grace College and Seminary (BA and MDiv), at Trinity Evangelical Divinity School (DMin), and most of all at God's School of Grace (not graduated yet), and to serve the Lord and grow together as pastor for over forty-six years with some very special congregations in Ohio, Indiana, and Pennsylvania. But most of all I have been blessed to have a God who so graciously loves me, saves me, and radically transforms me by the power of His Son Jesus living in me. (Galen Wiley).

Introduction

It's All about Jesus

As I look at all the ways that the Lord has transformed me over the years, I believe the central focus of it all has been learning that my life and ministry are all about Jesus – and not about me.

My life verse has been Philippians 3:10-11: "I want to know Christ and the power of His resurrection and the fellowship of sharing in His sufferings, becoming like Him in His death… to attain to the resurrection from the dead." However, my life experience has been the Lord taking me over and over again to the verses just before that to show me that the only way I can experience this reality is as I learn to put no confidence whatever in myself (my flesh or sinful nature – which Paul defines simply as ME in Romans 7:18) but instead to put all my confidence in Christ. This has been tough for me because I grew up in a pastor's home with godly parents who passionately loved the Lord, I accepted Jesus as my Lord and Savior at the age of seven and sought to walk with Him and dreamed of serving Him ever after that, I lived quite successfully by all the rules of the church, I went to an excellent Christian college and seminary to prepare myself (and was able to excel because of the academic abilities the Lord had given me), I went immediately into the pastorate upon graduation, I learned to push myself to work real hard at being the best pastor possible, and I attended all kinds of seminars and conferences and read all kinds of books and even took an advanced ministry degree in another outstanding seminary to prepare myself better to serve the Lord. Just like Paul, I had lots of reasons why I could be confident in myself, thinking that God could certainly use and bless someone like me – because I was working so hard to do everything "right" that I was supposed to do as a pastor in preaching the Word, loving God's people, and laying down my life for the Lord. In a sense I could almost think like Paul that in terms of the righteousness that is by law, I was pretty close to "faultless." But the Lord kept working so graciously to show me that all my accomplishments for Him are worthless compared to what He has accomplished and can accomplish in and through me. He has something so much more for us, something so much greater – that when we begin to experience it, everything we once thought was so exciting seems like so much rubbish in comparison. And I began to realize more and more that it's not about me and what all I can do for Jesus – it's about Jesus and what all He can do in and through me.

In 1976 the Lord took me through a life-altering experience. At the age of 30 I was diagnosed with coronary artery disease and was told that I would need open heart surgery (those were very rare at that time). And my wife was ready to deliver our third child at the same time. From the moment I was told the diagnosis, I had the sense that this was something so big that the Lord could do something super amazing in my life through this experience. It was while I was at Cleveland Clinic waiting (quite impatiently I must admit) for over a week for the surgery that the Lord dealt with me about the Biblical truth, "The just shall live by faith" (Romans 1:17). That was a real turning point in my life as I began to realize that just as I had been saved by faith in Jesus' work and not my own, even so I had to learn to live by faith in that same way.

Then in the 1980's the Lord used an advanced ministry degree program to push me into a study of the New Testament Mystery as a major project. I still don't know how I got to that focus – other than that the Lord graciously drew me to it (and He slammed the door shut on what I had initially planned). Through that study I concluded that God's NT Mystery was all about Jesus. And in particular it focused on the reality of Christ bringing every area of our lives as believers now into submission under His headship and someday the entire universe as well (Ephesians 1:9-11, 20-23) and on the reality of "Christ in you, the hope of glory" (Colossians 1:27). I was able to complete the project and submit the paper for the degree, but in another sense I was just beginning. The Lord has worked in my life profoundly ever since then to lead me to what this reality actually means for all my life and ministry.

So as I look back over the years, I see the Holy Spirit has been steadily leading me to one supreme passion of life – Jesus. It's all about Jesus. It is Christ living in me that is my hope of glory. And it is Christ living in those I love and minister to that is their only hope of glory as well!! He must increase; I must decrease. I must learn to put no confidence whatsoever in my flesh (NIV – sinful nature), that is in myself and what I have done or can do. Instead I must glory in Christ and put all my confidence in Him. And as I have slowly allowed the Spirit to do His work in me, I have found that all my accomplishments that I once thought were so special are actually so much rubbish, garbage, junk in comparison to the delight of knowing Jesus and of gaining all the things that He came to provide for me.

And so I invite you to join me in this pure delight of discovering all the awesome reality of God's mystery power unleashed through Jesus living and working in and through us for Him and His glory. It's all about Jesus.

PART ONE

The Person of God's Mystery Power

READING JESUS

Chapter 1

I have spent most of my life believing the absolute importance of reading the Bible to learn what God wants me to know. But I have become increasingly intrigued with the realization that God has an even more powerful way that He is speaking to me. That is Jesus!!!

In Hebrews 1, the author described how in the past God spoke to His people in many times and in many ways by the prophets. But in these last days God has spoken to us by His Son Jesus, who is "the radiance of God's glory and the exact representation of His being" (vv 1-3). It is just like John wrote that Jesus is the "Word of God" (John 1:1-14). Jesus came as the living Word of God, revealing to us God and His glory. In particular Jesus is God speaking to us about the fullness of the glory of God's grace and truth. And the only way we can "read" this fullness of grace and truth is simply by reading His Son Jesus as the Living Word of God.

Jesus is the ultimate way that God speaks to us today under the New Covenant. So we need to learn to read not only the written Word of God revealed through God's prophets and apostles but also the living Word of God revealed through God's Son. Reading the Bible is exciting, but reading Jesus is infinitely more exciting.

It is so exciting then to read Hebrews 2-4 from this perspective of Hebrews 1:1-3. We must pay much closer attention to what we have heard – of what God is speaking to us through Jesus. If Old Testament believers were judged for every violation and disobedience to what God spoke through His prophets, how shall we escape if we ignore such a great salvation that God is revealing to us through His Son Jesus (2:1-4)? Rather than focusing our attention on Moses, we must fix our thoughts on Jesus, the Apostle and High Priest whom we confess because He is so much greater than Moses (3:1-6). And the whole challenge of entering into God's rest is based upon our willingness to "HEAR GOD'S VOICE" as He speaks to us (3:7-4:11). The Old Testament believers did not hear or believe or obey what God spoke to them through Moses, so they did not enter into God's promised rest. So the only way we can enter God's promised rest for us today is as we "HEAR GOD'S VOICE" as He speaks to us through His Son Jesus – and believe and obey what God says. That is why we are told to "make every effort to enter that rest, so that no one will fall by following their example of disobedience" (4:11). We can only enjoy God's promised rest of His Great Salvation as we learn to HEAR what God is speaking to us through His Son Jesus.

And I believe that we should read Hebrews 4:12-16 in that same way. JESUS is the Word of God that is living and active, sharper than any double-edged sword, penetrating even to dividing soul and spirit, joints and marrow, and judging the thoughts and attitudes of the heart. Nothing in all creation is hidden from HIS sight, but everything is uncovered and laid bare before the eyes of HIM to whom we must give account. The written word of God can convict us to a limited degree, especially in matters of external behavior. But Jesus is the One who can penetrate to the thoughts and intentions of our heart. As we focus on Jesus and read Him as "the radiance of God's glory and the exact representation of His being" and as the full revelation of the glory of God in all His grace and truth, that is when we are truly convicted that we are sinners who fall so far short of the glory of God and who desperately need a Savior!! And that is when we will cry out to Jesus as our Great High Priest and come to Him at His throne of grace to receive mercy and find grace to help us in our time of need.

Possibly the author of Hebrews was still referring to this same reality of God speaking to us today through His Son Jesus when he concluded in 12:25, "See to it that you do not refuse Him who speaks. If they did not escape when they refused him who warned them on earth [Moses], how much less will we, if we turn away from Him [Jesus] who warns us from heaven?"

That is why in the early church they simply preached Jesus and the reality of His death and resurrection and exaltation to heaven!! For many years they didn't even have the New Testament Scriptures. All they had was Jesus and the good news that God's only Son had become flesh to dwell among us, so He could die for our sins and rise again and then go to heaven with all authority now in heaven and earth. They simply preached that Jesus could save any who would believe in Him and call on Him to save them. In the early church all they had was Jesus, the good news of what God was speaking to them through His Son. And when they referred to the Old Testament Scriptures it was primarily to validate that Jesus is truly God's promised Messiah and that we find life by faith in Him.

So as we look at the New Testament Scriptures, we need to see them simply as God using the apostles and prophets to write what God had revealed to them through Jesus. Many of them lived with Jesus for three years. They were there when He died on the cross, when He rose again, when He went back to heaven. They heard Him explain what all He had accomplished by His death and resurrection (Paul later met the Lord and received direct revelation from Him too). And they were sent out to tell the world what Jesus had told them and also what the Holy Spirit told them of how we can receive and enjoy this Great Salvation that is available to all who come to Jesus by faith and HEAR what God is speaking to them through His Son Jesus. So the New Testament is simply what they heard God speak to them through Jesus (directly or through the Holy Spirit). And they wrote down those truths, so that we can understand what they heard and then learn how to HEAR God ourselves today as Jesus speaks to us by the Holy Spirit to lead us into this Great Salvation He came to provide for us. The Scriptures are BIG in God's plan, but His Son Jesus is BIGGER!

We learned in seminary days how to do careful "exegesis" of the Bible, as we would carefully study the written Word of God and make sure we understood and explained it accurately and correctly. Now I realize that it is infinitely more important to learn how to do careful "EXEJESUS" of the Son, as we carefully study the living Word of God and make sure we understand and explain Him accurately and correctly. Now we must still be sure to handle the written Word of God carefully as well. In fact, Paul explained in 2 Timothy 3:15, that it is the Holy Scriptures that have the power to "make us wise for salvation through faith in Christ Jesus." And Paul was referring to the Old Testament Scriptures that Timothy had as a child. They simply told that the Christ was coming someday. How much greater power do the New Testament Scriptures have as they tell us how Jesus came and what He did for us so He can save us and give us life as we come to Him by faith as Lord and Savior of every area of our lives.

I am more convinced than ever that if we truly want to find and enjoy this Great Salvation that God has provided for us through His Son Jesus, we have to learn to HEAR God speaking to us through His Son Jesus and we must believe and obey what God is saying to us. The Bible is so important because that is where we learn about Jesus and how to hear what God is saying to us through Him. But we must go beyond reading the Bible as the written Word of God and learn to read Jesus as the living Word of God – because only Jesus can save us and set us free to find and enjoy life to the full now and forever!! I must admit, it is easier to pick up the Bible and read it than to look to Jesus and read Him. And it is easier to think that I have done everything I need to do when I read the Bible and pray at the start of the day than when I come to Jesus to hear Him speak to me about what He wants to say to me for that day.

So I believe that God wants us to hear Him speak to us through His Son – and to simply believe and obey whatever He is speaking to us!! We must learn to READ JESUS!! That is when Jesus will save us and set us free, so we can live life to the full not only in this lifetime but also for an eternity. We must do careful "exegesis" of the written Word of God because this is how the Holy Spirit leads us to Jesus and makes us wise for the salvation He came to bring us. But then we must also do careful "exejesus" of the living Word of God because that is how we come to Jesus and find and live LIFE TO THE FULL IN HIM!!

THE PATH TO LIFE
Chapter 2

I still remember vividly the time when I was reading John 5:39-40 in my personal devotions, and the Holy Spirit convicted me deeply that I needed a major transformation in my life and ministry. Just like the religious leaders of Jesus' day, I had bought Satan's lie that diligently studying Scripture is what leads me to find and live life to the full. And I thought that is how I could lead my family and my congregation as well to find and live life to the full – by teaching them more and more of God's truth revealed in the Bible. But as I read that the purpose of Scripture is to tell me about Jesus so I can come to Him to have life, that is when the light finally dawned on me that life is in the Son not in the Scripture.

There is the danger of trying to find life through Scripture without Jesus: I had committed my life to studying the Bible, and I was a part of a Fellowship of churches that had committed itself to the same thing. We loved what Jesus said in John 8:32, "You will know the truth and the truth will set you free." And to us that truth was the truth of the Bible. So our job was simply to study and preach the truth of God's written Word, and all our lives would be changed. The problem was that all too often people's lives weren't being changed. In fact, some of the people who were the most mean, selfish and demanding people I knew were people who had studied and mastered the Bible and sometimes were even teaching it to others. That was hard to understand.

Jesus spoke these words to the religious leaders of His day who had mastered not only the Jewish Scriptures but also the writings of the rabbis expanding on the Old Testament and all its laws. They knew the Book and the books. And they taught everyone else to do the same thing. The reason they studied the Scripture so diligently was because they thought that they would find life in that study – for this lifetime and for an eternity. They believed the path to life was studying and mastering the Bible as God's Word. And they taught others to believe the same thing. But I realized that these Jewish leaders who studied and taught all about the coming Messiah ended up crucifying the Messiah that God sent to them to give them life, the Messiah they had studied and taught about all their lives. They had mastered the Book, but they ended up killing the Master of the Book. And they missed out on God's life in this lifetime and forever (unless they repented and came to Jesus).

But what really convicted me was that Jesus said they were not coming to Him to have life. I still remember all those Scriptures going through my mind that said that life is in Jesus. Jesus is the One who came to bring us life. It is faith in Jesus, not the Scripture that brings us life. God so loved the world that He sent His Son not Scripture to give us life (John 3:16; 10:10; 14:6; 20:31). Now the Scriptures are so important because as Jesus said, "The Scriptures testify about Me." The entire Bible tells us about Jesus. The Old Testament said He was coming and why we needed Him to come. The Gospels said He came. The rest of the New Testament tells us why He came and what He did and how we can find life in Him now and forever. That is why we have to do more than just study the Bible if we want life. We have to do more than just teach people the truths of the Bible if we want to lead them to life. We have to come to Jesus and we have to lead others to Jesus. Only Jesus can bring us life.

This is a huge danger for those of us who have grown up in conservative, evangelical churches. We have been taught that the solution for every problem is simply to study the Bible to find the right verses to memorize, believe and obey. And the job of the church is simply to teach everyone all the facts of the Bible, so they will know all the right Bible verses also. All too often we measure our maturity and the maturity of others on how many Bible facts we know. All too often we think we have listened to a sermon or Bible study if we write notes and learn something new we didn't know before. One of Satan's master deceptions is to make us think that the path to life is studying diligently the Bible and teaching others to do the same. We must remember that the ultimate purpose of the Bible is always to lead us to Jesus, so that we can find life in Him – life to the full now and forever!! So if we ever study and teach the Bible just to learn the Bible without coming to Jesus, we fall into Satan's trap.

However, I also remember how excited I was when the Spirit reminded me of what Paul wrote in 2 Timothy 3:15-17. In verses 16-17 Paul told us that we must treat God's Word seriously – because this is God's Book!! This Book is God-breathed. God the Holy Spirit wrote this Book. What was originally written in Hebrew, Aramaic, and Greek was precisely what God wanted written even down to the words and the letters making up those words. God is God. This Book tells us about God. This Book tells us all the absolute truth about God we need to know, including absolute right and wrong. This Book tells us how to live so we will be ready for that judgment day when we stand before God as the Final Judge. And this Book was given to change our lives. The Holy Spirit wrote His masterpiece to lead us to live again in God's truth that is always profitable for teaching, rebuking, correcting, training in righteousness, so we can be complete, equipped for every good work. One of the most important decisions we will ever make is to accept that God is God, He has written this Book, and He gave it to us to change our lives!! This means that we do not live by human teachings, theologies and traditions nor by human rules, regulations and rituals – but by God's Word.

But here is what I missed for years – this Book was ultimately written to make us wise for the salvation that is by faith in Jesus (verse 15). The real, dynamite power of the Bible is to tell us how to find salvation by faith in Jesus that will deliver us from death and give us the gift of life to the full now in this lifetime and forever!! And this life comes by one way and one alone – by faith in Christ Jesus. This life is always in the SON (1 John 5:11-12)!! So this is the ultimate purpose of the Bible – to make us wise, to give us the understanding, to teach us all the truths of how to find and live salvation by faith in Jesus. And I believe that even all the work of Scriptures described in verses 16-17 is ultimately through the power of Jesus working in us – Jesus is the One teaching us truth, convicting us of error, leading us back to the truth, training us in righteousness, and equipping us for every good work! That is the power of Jesus saving us and setting us free to live life to the full!!

There is the danger of trying to find life through Jesus without Scripture: Now the Bible is very clear that God has the right to define the path to find life in Jesus – and He has defined it in His Book. In the context of Romans 9-11 God explained that there is no other way!!! It doesn't matter how sincere we are or how hard we may work or even if we may be a part of God's special chosen Jewish people who are keeping the Law of Moses, all that matters is God showing mercy (see Romans 9:16). And God has determined that He shows mercy only to those who come to Jesus and live by faith in Him and Him alone – as defined in God's Book. There is no other way. This is why it is so important that we must not follow other people's plans and ideas!!! God is God!! And only His way works!! And He has defined His way in this Book!! Now fortunately He has made the path so simple that a child can follow that path (Romans 10:9-13 – <u>confess</u> Jesus is Lord, <u>believe</u> that He died for our sins and rose again, and <u>ask</u> Jesus to save us).

So if we want to find and enjoy the life that Jesus came to bring us, we must come precisely according to what God has determined and described in His Book. This Book tells us how to come to Jesus by faith to receive this salvation He came to provide for us. This Book tells us precisely how this gift of salvation works in delivering us from sin, Satan, death and hell and setting us free to live in God's holiness and righteousness and truth. It's exciting to know that Jesus is more than able to do His work in His way and in His time in anyone who comes to Him simply by faith as defined by the truth of this Book!!

I believe there is a second great danger that is uniquely facing those of us who grow up in the evangelical church today. It is that we live in a post-modern world where we are taught there is no absolute truth and all religions are equally valid and everyone has to choose whatever path they want to follow. And it doesn't matter what you choose because all the paths end up at the same place in the end. This has led many Christians and churches to downplay the study and teaching of the truths of the Bible and to say that all that matters is that we love God and one another. We can all decide for ourselves what God is like and how we find life in Him ("My God would never send anyone to hell. My God is love. We are all God's children no matter what we have done."). The path to life is simply warm fuzzy moments with the Jesus we want Him to be. It can even be just nice songs we sing and experiences we enjoy and emotions we feel. It's all about love, love, love.

The first great danger was thinking we can find life in the study of the Scripture without Jesus. But the second great danger is thinking we can find life in Jesus without Scripture – the Jesus we create the way we want Him to be. We must never forget that God is God, and God has defined in this Book exactly who Jesus is and how Jesus works and how we must come by faith to Jesus and bow before Him as Savior and Lord of all if we ever want to receive and enjoy His salvation giving us life to the full now and forever!!

The path to life is very clear – the Bible leads us to Jesus, and Jesus leads us to life. We must take this Book seriously that God has written to us. We must refuse to allow anyone or anything to deceive us into some Satanic counterfeit. This Book was written to lead us to come to Jesus as the only One who is able to save us from death and set us free for life!! Only Jesus can give us life. And this life He gives is awesome!! It is life to the full now in this lifetime and someday forever in the New Heaven and the New Earth!!

For those who are searching, those who feel something is missing, those who want to find life to the full, those who want everything that God has for them, those who want to shake free from all of the ways that Satan is deceiving them and messing up their lives, we must simply come to Jesus!! Not our Jesus in our way. But God's Jesus in God's way. We must simply come to Jesus by faith according to the truth defined in this Book – and receive and enjoy His salvation bringing us life to the full now and forever, life that is both spiritual and physical as well.

GOD'S MYSTERY STORY
Chapter 3

Early in the 1980's God excited me about something from His Word that started me on a radical transformation of my life and ministry – God's New Testament Mystery. As I studied the 27 or 28 times the word "mystery" is used in the New Testament, I concluded that God was talking about something very special. Most of these passages talked about God's mystery (things unknowable apart from God's revelation) as something totally hidden before the death and resurrection of Christ, but then revealed for all the saints through the apostles and prophets in the early church, and completed during the future tribulation when what is now mystery will be fully revealed. It is still "mystery" today because only believers will understand it and even then only as they allow God to reveal it to them. There are a few passages using the word in more general ways, but most of them focus on this very special mystery God revealed for us who live under the New Covenant.

As a result of my study, I concluded that the entire focus of God's Mystery Story is Jesus. Of course, the Old Testament predicted that Jesus as their Messiah would come and die and rise again. That's what Jesus could explain to His disciples after His resurrection (Luke 24:25-26, 44-46). God had also revealed that this Messiah would rule over the Kingdom of Israel that would bring peace to the entire world. But what God had not revealed was that this Messiah would fulfill the law and bring in a new covenant of grace where now we are saved and live no longer under the Law of Moses but now by faith and faith alone in Jesus as Lord and Savior. So Jesus is God's Mystery, Jesus not as King of Israel in a literal kingdom on earth but Jesus as Lord of all in a spiritual kingdom over all who will bow the knee before Him and by faith accept and follow Him as their personal Lord and Savior.

I concluded that there are two passages that best define the essence of God's New Testament Mystery: 1) God's will is that all things in heaven and earth are to be brought into submission under Jesus' control (Ephesians 1:9-11, 19-23). We as believers choose to do that now in this lifetime, as we allow Jesus as Lord to transform us radically in every area of our lives. Unbelievers will someday bow the knee, but then it will be too late (Philippians 2:9-11). This is why the heart of being a Christian is that we choose now to bow the knee and confess with our mouth and our lives that truly Jesus is Lord. We submit to Him as Lord in everything, as we allow Him to bring every area of our lives into submission under His control. 2) We experience every facet of God's salvation through the power of His Son Jesus, as He comes to live inside of us, as our only hope of glory (Colossians 1:24-2:3). The only way we can ever fulfill God's will that every area of our life would come under the control of Jesus as Lord is through the power and reality of Christ living in us. Jesus as the Son of God is seated in the heavenlies at the right hand of God with all authority in heaven and earth, but yet He lives in us (in the person of the Holy Spirit)!!! So we experience all of God's salvation by faith in Jesus, as He unleashes in us all the power of His death, all the power of His resurrection, and all the power of His exaltation. We need to remember that this is mystery: this is something we would never guess or figure out apart from God's revelation. But by faith we believe it is reality – because God says it is!!

In Colossians 1:24-2:3 Paul explains very clearly how radically our lives will change when we allow God to unleash in us all of His mystery power that is available in Jesus. Christ in us is our ultimate and only hope of glory. And there are three big ways where God's mystery power will radically change our lives as it is unleashed in us.

PERFECTION – The goal of Christ living and working in us is to lead us toward perfection or maturity (1:28), where we become more and more like Christ all the time in holiness and righteousness in the truth (Colossians 1:21-22; Ephesians 4:24). We are tempted to think that God cares about how much theology we have mastered, Scriptures we have memorized, good works we have done, ministries we have performed. But God cares so much more about how we are becoming more and more like Jesus on the inside as well as the outside. God wants us personally, as families and as a church to be growing toward perfection or maturity, becoming more and more like Jesus.

That is why Paul simply proclaimed Christ. He was admonishing (warning, instructing) everyone and teaching everyone in all wisdom (God's wisdom, not man's). And as Paul wrote in 1 Corinthians 1-3, Jesus is the power of God and the wisdom of God. It is Jesus Christ and Him crucified (now risen, exalted, and living for us and in us) that is God's ultimate wisdom that confounds all the wisdom of this world. So we simply proclaim Christ.

This has been a revolutionary truth in my life. The way we learn to grow up in Jesus and the way we help others to grow up in Jesus – is by letting Christ living in us radically change our lives and set us free to become like Him in holiness and righteousness in the truth!! Only Jesus can make us perfect!! So we proclaim/preach Jesus!! Nothing more and nothing less!!

I marvel at how great this perfection really is. The immaturity and imperfection of sin and lawlessness always lead to Satanic bondage, tyranny, corruption, destruction, death. In contrast, the maturity and perfection of holiness and righteousness in truth always lead to Jesus' freedom, control, health, strength, stability, joy, peace, life. Satan always steals, kills, and destroys, but Jesus always brings us life to the full – now and forever (John 10:10). This means Jesus sets us free from all the sins of the past, all the bad choices we have made, all the ways our emotions have gotten all messed up, all the horrible ways Satan has deceived us with his lies and lusts (John 8:44). And now Jesus is setting us free to think, talk, live, relate, dream and desire in right ways, the ways that are truly good, the ways He created us to live. And these ways work – so good!!

As I look at my life, my marriage, my family, my ministry, I am so thrilled to see and enjoy all the ways that Jesus has been maturing me to be and do what is holy and righteous according to God's truth. I still have a long way to go, but I am so thrilled to see how far Jesus has led me already and to know He will keep working on me until someday in heaven the job is done.

POWER – After living so much of my life thinking it was up to me to make myself holy and righteous on the inside, one of the most thrilling truths I have learned from God's Word is that the power is all of Jesus. That's why Paul said here that the power to proclaim Christ and to lead himself and everyone else toward that goal of perfection and maturity in Christ is the power of Christ living in us. Paul said we can live "according to Christ's energy which is energizing in us in dynamite power!!" (1:29).

Let's get real – it is impossible for us to make ourselves truly holy and righteous on the inside and outside. Sometimes we can control some bad behavior in some circumstances, but the old sinful nature keeps bursting forth in the most embarrassing times and ways. It is often easier to control ourselves in public where we are trying to impress people; but when we are at home with our mate and family, that's where things can blow up so quickly. Or when we are all alone and no one sees, that's when we can give in to some secret patterns of thought and action and emotions that Satan has so subtly built into our lives. It is such good news that Jesus Himself is the One working in us to make us perfect just like He is.

And the power is all of Him!! It is His energy that energizes in us in dynamite power – to make us perfect like He is!!

But it is important to remember that Paul described our part of the process. He explained that he was laboring (becoming weary or tired; working hard, toiling) and striving (used in an athletic contest or in warfare, "to fight, struggle"; we get word "agonizing" from this). But he was doing this totally according to the power of Christ working in him. In 1 Corinthians 15:10, Paul said he worked harder than all of them, "yet not I but the grace of God with me." In Philippians 2:12-13, Paul talked about us working out with fear and trembling our salvation that God is working in us (to will and to do of His good pleasure). Jesus has all power in heaven and earth, so He can make us truly perfect in every area of our lives. But the choice is still ours whether or not we will choose to do and be what Jesus is working in us to do and be. The power is all of Jesus, but the choice is ours to work out what He is working in us.

We need to remember from Colossians 1:15-20 how great His power really is – Jesus as God the Son has created and controls the entire universe!! So He is more than able to handle whatever we face and to radically change our lives to become more and more like Him. One trap Satan uses is to get us to think that our bondages are so strong, our sin so terrible, our past so messed up that even Jesus can never set us free and make us holy and righteous in truth. So we give up and decide we can never change. Another huge trap Satan uses is to get us to think that we can handle this in our power, our brilliance, and our hard work – or in someone else's. All too often we end up going from one "solution" to another. And when one doesn't work, we just assume that we have to find a better "solution" and just try harder!! But we have Christ living in us, and He has all the power He needs to break every bondage and to make us truly holy and righteous just like He is. Our job is simply to believe He can do it and let Him work, as we work hard at doing and being whatever He leads us to do and be, thinking whatever He gives us to think, living however He leads us to live, and ministering however He leads us to minister – all through His power He unleashes in our lives.

We need to get excited about the incomprehensible power of Christ unleashed and working in us leading us to perfection. When the power is ours, we always fail over and over again in constant imperfection. And we live in fear knowing that our power will always run out and we'll end up in failure. But when we are living by the power of Christ living and working in us, that is an infinite power that will never run out. And we can go from one victory to another, always toward perfection!! This can help us to face whatever we are facing today and whatever we may face tomorrow in the confidence that Christ in us is big enough and strong enough to give us everything we need for us to be and do everything He wants for us.

WISDOM – Paul also wanted the Colossian believers to have the full riches of complete understanding unto a knowledge of the mystery of God, Christ – in whom are hidden all the treasures of wisdom and knowledge (2:2-3). The Bible as the written Word of God is God's partial revelation to us, pointing us to Jesus. But Jesus as the living Word of God is God's ultimate, complete revelation to us (John 1:1-18; Colossians 2:17; Hebrews 1:1-3). And once we come to Jesus, that is when He opens our eyes to see and our ears to hear and our minds to conceive things we have never seen, heard, nor conceived before (1 Corinthians 2:9). All the treasures of wisdom and knowledge are hidden in Jesus. And they are all ours to find and enjoy.

This means that these are hidden treasures that we can find only in Jesus. This means that all the professors, philosophers, psychologists, entertainers, educators, and politicians don't have the final answers to life. This also means that we might study the

Bible 24/7, we might learn to use the Greek and Hebrew, and we might accumulate all kinds of degrees in advanced education, but we may still not find God's ultimate treasures that are hidden in Christ. Paul warned us in the rest of Colossians 2 of the danger of living according to the philosophies, teachings, and rules and regulations of mere men (or even living according to Old Testament law). There is a feeling of pride and arrogance in all of our knowledge. But we are missing out on the real life that is only in Christ – where all the genuine treasures of wisdom and knowledge are hidden.

We need to get excited about all the wisdom and knowledge that are hidden in Jesus. We live in a world deceived by Satan's lies and lusts. This is his kingdom of darkness. And he has blinded the minds of those who do not believe (2 Corinthians 4:3-4). We also live as a part of a church that has been confused and deceived by Satan and his cheap counterfeit Christianity for almost 2000 years. Now we all hate to be scammed, taken, deceived, ripped off, but that is what Satan is doing all the time through the world and even through the church. But when we come to Jesus and let Him lead us into all these treasures of wisdom and knowledge hidden in Him, He transforms us by the renewing of our minds as He unravels all the layers upon layers of lies and deceptions Satan has built into our minds and leads us into the fullness of knowing what God's good and pleasing and perfect will is (Romans 12:1-2). We come to know the truth, and the truth sets us free, when Jesus is the One leading us to the truth that He is (John 8:31-36).

What a mystery! What a reality! Christ in us, the hope of glory, the glory of His perfection, the glory of His power, the glory of His wisdom. We find all of this in the Person of Jesus Christ. Jesus is God's eternal Son, fully God and fully man. He is alive, and He lives in us. And He loves us. And we can trust His love. That is mystery! That is reality!

Jesus is God's Mystery Story. Jesus is God's one and only plan to save us from death and give us life!! But the decision is still ours. We can keep trying to save ourselves. We can keep thinking that others can save us – Hollywood, Washington, Harvard, Madison Avenue, even the church. Or we can dare to believe that Jesus can and Jesus will when we come to Him in simple faith!!

It's an amazing mystery that the God of eternity actually wants to save us and give us this amazing gift of life so much that He sent His one and only Son Jesus down here to die on a cross for us and to rise again. He invites us to accept this gift simply by believing that Jesus is God's one and only Son and the Savior of all who come to Him. And then He wants us to discover and enjoy all the infinite riches of this gift through the power of Christ living in us as our hope of glory and bringing every area of our lives into submission under His headship!! It is Christ alive and living in us who is able to lead us to His perfection, to His power, and to all the treasures of His wisdom and knowledge. It is Mystery, but God will unleash that Mystery in all who continue simply to come to Jesus and believe in Him as the One who is alive and living in us, as our only hope of glory – now and forever!!

PART TWO

The Greatness of God's Mystery Power

CRUCIFIXION POWER
Chapter 4

We probably all remember things in our past that we did that were bad. Or maybe things that weren't actually bad, but our choices brought pain to other people. Or maybe someone else did bad things to us, and they blamed us for making them do them, and we still wonder if maybe it was our fault. We probably all have many memories that still haunt us and make us feel guilty.

Guilt can have a powerful effect in our lives. Often we feel we have to do all kinds of good things to make up for the bad things we did. Or we feel we are a bad person, and we can't be forgiven. And we assume that everyone remembers us for what we did wrong. Maybe we think that even God can't forgive us, and we'll pay for eternity. I suspect that many people keep a distance from God and the Bible because they feel guilty before God, so they want to hide in the bushes just like Adam and Eve did in the garden. And of course many addictions and mental disorders are the direct result of guilt.

Now the reality is that we are all sinners, and therefore all guilty before God (according to Romans 3:19 the law shows that we are all guilty or accountable before God – "under punishment"). And the penalty for sin is death in this lifetime and forever, both spiritual and physical (Romans 6:23). So we really should feel guilty before God – because we are!!

The amazing truth at the heart of the Gospel is that Jesus died for our sins (1 Corinthians 15:3-5). God loved us so much that He sent His Son into our world to take on a human body, live a perfect life, and then choose to take our sins upon Himself and die for our sins on the cross. Jesus was fully God and fully man. As man He could die, as God He could die for all the sins of the world. He had never sinned, so He did not have to die. But He chose to take our sins upon Himself, so He could die in our place and take the punishment for our sins upon Himself and pay the price for our sins in full. So now He can deliver us from the power of sin, Satan, death, and hell.

That's why Paul wrote in 1 Corinthians 1:18-2:5 that his whole message was Jesus Christ and Him crucified. The message of the cross is the power of God and the wisdom of God that can save any who believe. And the way to receive God's gift of eternal life is simply to confess with our mouth that Jesus is Lord, to believe that Jesus died for our sins and that He arose from the dead, and to call on His Name for salvation (Romans 10:9-13).

So the power of the death of Jesus is the power to deliver us from our sins. I have become very excited that this power goes way beyond something we experience just on the day we come to Jesus for salvation. It is a power Jesus wants to unleash every day of our lives. I have been so blessed personally to see some of the amazing ways that Jesus deals with our sin as we come to the cross and let Him unleash in us the power of the cross.

FORGIVEN – This is the amazing truth that all our sins are forgiven when we accept Jesus as Lord and Savior. It was our sin that made us guilty before a holy God and put us under the judgment of death. But Jesus paid the price for our sins in full, so He can forgive us completely. Our record is expunged and wiped clean; the penalty has been paid in full. Now legally God can look at us as if we had never sinned. Legally, all our sins past, present and future were paid for at the cross and forgiven when we accepted Jesus as our Lord and Savior. It doesn't matter how much we have sinned, how terribly we have sinned, how long we have sinned, when we accept Jesus we are forgiven in full for all our sins past, present, and future. What a relief that is!!!

Whenever Satan tries to make us feel guilty for our sins, we can remember the cross and know we are forgiven!!!

FREED – But God loves us too much just to forgive us and then let us still be enslaved by our sins. Just think of how as parents we love our children too much to let them play with fire or with rattlesnakes or toilet bowl cleaner. When we come to Jesus and ask Him to save us, we are in an instant forgiven of all our sins. But we are still messed up on the inside with sinful patterns of thought, action, words and relationships with God and with other people.

The reason it takes so long for Jesus to free us from these old ways of thinking and living is that Jesus works only as we let Him work. Before we came to Jesus, Satan had built a web of interlocking, twisted, convoluted patterns of his lies and lusts that had become the very essence of who we are (John 8:44). And each sin pattern led to all kinds of consequences in our lives in all kinds of spiritual pain, disease, and death. For example, my sin of legalism led to patterns of perfectionism, fear of failure, fear of what people think, feelings of living as a slave under law trying to earn God's love rather than living as a son enjoying His love, feeling guilty if I'm not doing something productive, feeling like I have never done enough, and many other things. And even after we come to Jesus, we let go so very slowly. So Jesus can work only as we let Him. It is a lifetime process for us to give God total control to transform us by the renewing of our minds to know and do His good, pleasing and perfect will (Romans 12:1-2).

It is the power of the cross that is able to set us free from these old ways of thinking, acting, talking and relating, so that now He can teach us His new ways to live. Jesus is able to free us not only from the sin and deception patterns of the past but also from all the ways those patterns have shaped and twisted our mind and actions. Jesus died for our sins not only so we can be forgiven of our sins but also so we can be freed from the power of those sins in our lives and from all the ramifications of that power. It doesn't matter how much we have sinned, how terribly we have sinned, how long we have sinned, once we have been forgiven of our sins, Jesus now has all the power He needs to free us from the power of those sins in every part of our lives.

FORGOTTEN – I suspect there is one final area where Satan is still trying to keep a stronghold in my life – and maybe in yours as well. But this is also a huge area where Jesus wants to free us. Our sins can also be totally forgotten!!

Under the New Covenant of grace God says, "For I will forgive their wickedness and will remember their sins no more" (Hebrews 8:12; 10:17). This is part of the thrilling upgrade that New Covenant grace brings over Old Covenant law (Hebrews 10:1-4 tells us that law constantly reminds us of how guilty we are). God does NOT (emphatic in Greek) remember our sins any longer. The word for "remember" is the word for "to remember, remind oneself, keep in mind, make mention of, care for, be concerned about." The Bible teaches us that Satan is the slanderer (meaning of "devil"), the accuser of the believers, and he accuses us before God in heaven day and night (Revelation 12:10). So Satan keeps condemning us and making us feel guilty before God all the time. No matter how fully we have been forgiven and how completely we have been freed, Satan keeps reminding us of ours sins and failures of the past and making us feel guilty, worthless, failures, under God's judgment, and under people's judgment too.

But God says that under New Testament grace, He forgets our sins. Satan reminds!!! But God forgets!!! God's love is the antidote for guilt. God not only forgives, He forgets. He not only wipes the slate clean, He throws the slate away! Now this does not mean we can go ahead and sin deliberately because God doesn't care or know. That puts Satan back in control and puts us back under

God's judgment – until we repent and confess that sin and bring it back to Jesus to free us from that sin (Hebrews 10:26-31). And this does not mean we can't refer to our sin to show off how great God's grace really is (like Paul did in 1 Timothy 1:12-17 and like God will do at the Judgment Seat of Christ as in 1 Corinthians 3:12-15 and 2 Corinthians 5:10). In fact, our sins forgiven, freed and forgotten are actually ways we can show off the awesome glory of God's grace now and forever (Ephesians 1:6, 12, 14; 2:7; 3:20-21).

But God forgets and we should too!! This is what God accomplished for us when Jesus died on the cross for our sins once for all (Hebrews 10:12-18). God says that now He will <u>NOT</u> remember our sins and lawless deed any longer!! And we should not either!! Satan will keep trying to remind us of our sins and of the sins of others. But God does not remember them, and He tells us not to remember them either. God says, "Forget it!!!!" Satan says, "Remember it!!!" And it is simply our choice who we will listen to.

God wants us to let go of our memories and guilt from the past. With my legalism, Jesus not only forgave me and freed me from my legalism but He also wants to help me "forget" the emotions and the guilt and the sense of failure from that sin. I fear that I have ignored this area of Jesus' work in my life more than I realize. All too easily I let Satan remind me of past failures and keep me feeling like a failure, a disappointment to God, insecure, inadequate, fearing that I will continue to fail and disappoint God, and feeling like I can never break free from my legalism and all its power in my life. Jesus does not want us feeling guilty about our sins and feeling like a failure, defeated, a nobody, a disaster, someone that God can never use. That's part of why He went to a cross and died for our sins, so we can forget our sins!!! God says He does not remember them against us now or ever!!! He has forgotten them!! So God does not want us to focus on our sin and all the pain that Satan brought into our lives and the lives of others we have hurt. Instead God wants us to focus on how He in His grace has forgiven us and freed us from all our sins - and how He wants to help us now to forget them as well!!!

It doesn't matter how much we have sinned, how terribly we have sinned, how long we have sinned, once we have been forgiven of our sins and freed from our sins, Jesus wants to wash away all those memories, all that guilt, all that condemnation that so devastates us. Jesus wants us to forget the past just as He has and live for the future of what He can and will do in us as we follow Him as Lord into the new life He has provided for us. I love what Paul wrote in Romans 5:20-21, "But where sin increased, grace increased all the more, so that, just as sin reigned in death, so also grace might reign through righteousness to bring eternal life through Jesus Christ our Lord." I want that life to the full where I forget the sins of the past and live in the anticipation of the righteousness and victory I can have in Christ.

This is the power of the cross – all our sins are forgiven, freed, forgotten now and forever! All our sins past, present, future are forgiven, expunged, the record wiped clean! And from all the bondages those sins brought into our lives, we can be freed, delivered, rescued, chains broken, strongholds torn down, prison cells opened. And all the memories, the haunting guilt, the sense of condemnation, the feelings of failure can be washed away in the precious blood of Jesus, so that now we can focus on what we are becoming in Jesus.

One of my favorite verses is 1 Corinthians 6:11. After listing some of the sins that enslave us and keep us from enjoying heaven as God's kingdom forever, Paul turns and says, "And that is what some of you were. But you were washed, you were sanctified, you were justified in the Name of the Lord Jesus." These are all past tense verbs. We were justified (declared righteous), we were sanctified (made holy), and we were washed (cleansed of all the dirt left behind). There's a chance that justified = forgiven, sanctified = freed, and washed = forgotten (washed or cleansed even from the memories, the guilt, and the sense of condemnation and impending doom). When we come to Jesus as our Lord and Savior, God no longer calls us sinners but now He calls us saints. He no longer calls us enemies but now He calls us His family forever!!! He loves us so much!! And He is so thrilled with what we are allowing Jesus to do in our lives – in forgiving, freeing, forgetting all our sins, in justifying, sanctifying, washing us!!!

This is the power of the cross for any who come to Jesus and ask Him to save them. It doesn't matter how much we have sinned, how terribly we have sinned, how long we have sinned, all we have to do is to come to Jesus and the power of the cross. Jesus Christ took all our sins to that cross and paid the price in full. So now anyone who will turn to Jesus and ask Him to save them and become their Lord and Savior, all their sins past, present and future will be fully and completely forgiven, freed, and forgotten forever! Jesus died for our sins, so we can find freedom from our sins now and forever!

Here is a partial list of some of the things Jesus accomplished for us when He died on the cross:

1. Christ died to deal with our sins
   a. Matthew 1:21; John 1:29; 1 Corinthians 15:3; 2 Corinthians 5:21; Hebrews 10:26-28 (about 40 places in NT that connect Christ's death and our sins).
   b. We bring Him great glory and joy when we bring Him our sin and let Him save us (1 Timothy 1:12-17; Luke 15:1-32).
2. Christ died to deliver us from death
   a. John 3:14-16, 36; 5:24; 10:10. The wages of sin is death, so by delivering us from sin He delivers us from death (Romans 3:23; 6:23). He also delivers us from Satan who has the power of death and from the fear of death that Satan

uses to enslave us (1 Corinthians 15:25-26; Hebrews 2:14-15).
   b. Jesus wants to deliver us not only from death in an eternal hell but also from corruption and death in this lifetime and from all the spiritual disease and pain involved in that dying process.
3. Christ died to reconcile us to God
   a. Romans 5:1-11; 2 Corinthians 5:14-21; Ephesians 2:1-22; Colossians 1:19-22; 1 Peter 3:18; 1 John 1:4-10. God welcomes us back into His family now and forever. We are no longer enemies under the wrath of God; now we are family under His love forever.
   b. God wants us to relax and enjoy being His family again (Luke 15:11-32; John 17:20-23; Romans 8:12-17; Galatians 4:1-7).
4. Christ died as the power of God to draw us back to God
   a. John 6:44; 12:31-32; 3:14-17; Romans 2:4; 1 John 4:9-10, 19; 2 Corinthians 5:14-15.
   b. That is why we preach Jesus Christ and Him crucified as the power and wisdom of God to draw people back to God (1Corinthians 1:17-2:5).
5. Christ died to teach us what love really is
   a. John 3:16-17; Romans 5:6-8; 1 John 4:7-10; Matthew 22:37-40; John 13:34-35. There is no greater love than God sending His Son and Jesus being willing to lay down His life for us.
   b. The more we are filled by the Spirit the more we will love like Christ loves (Galatians 5:22; 1 John 4:7-21). We will love God first (John 14:15-31) and one another second (John 13:34-35) just like Christ loves.
6. Christ died so we can die to ourselves
   a. Matthew 16:24-25; Luke 14:26-33; Romans 6:1-11; 12:1-2; Galatians 2:19-20; 2 Corinthians 4:11; Philippians 3:10-11.
   b. We die to self, so we can live unto God in a phenomenally greater life (Matthew 19:27-30; Philippians 2:5-11; 3:10-11; Hebrews 12:1-2).
7. Christ died to fulfill the law and deliver us from its power
   a. Galatians 3:10-14; Ephesians 2:14-16; Colossians 2:13-15; 1 Corinthians 15:56-57.

    b. We are no longer living under law; now we are living under grace – and fulfilling the righteous requirements of the law through Christ living in us (Romans 6:14-15; 8:4; Colossians 1:27-29).
8. Christ died to disarm Satan and crush him under our feet
    a. Genesis 3:15; Colossians 2:15; Hebrews 2:14-15; Romans 16:20; Galatians 6:14; Ephesians 1:20-23.
    b. That is why we can march in victory now in the confidence of our victory in Christ (2 Corinthians 2:14). (Reminder that we are powerless in ourselves – Acts 19:13-16).
9. Christ died to deliver us from our flesh
    a. Colossians 2:9-13; Romans 6:6; Galatians 5:24; Ephesians 4:22-24; Colossians 3:9-10 (Romans 7:1-25; 8:1-8; Galatians 5:16-26; 6:7-8 for more on flesh).
    b. The blood of Christ cleanses our consciences from dead works (the sacrifices and actions under the law) so that we may serve the living God (Hebrews 9:14).
    c. That is why we must not put any confidence in the flesh for any of life and ministry – but in Christ only (Philippians 3:3-14).

RESURRECTION POWER
Chapter 5

One thing I have learned in life is that there's a right way and a wrong way to do things. And it's better to do things right the first time – than to do it wrong and try to straighten it out later. I'm a "do-it-yourself" kind of guy. That means I've made a lot of mistakes, but I try to learn from my mistakes and then figure out how to get it right. Now today we have the internet and You Tube where we can learn from others who have already learned from their mistakes – and hopefully get it right the first time ourselves.

But there are some things in life where the impact of our decisions is profound for the rest of our lives. For example, who we marry or how we parent our children or whether or not we accept Jesus as Lord and Savior (that has eternal consequences). Fortunately, the Bible says that Jesus has the power to help us get it right, including in these big decisions of life that have so much impact for now and for an eternity.

Romans 6 is one of the most powerful passages talking about how Jesus can help us get it right in life!! There are two key words in this passage that describe what we will find as we allow Jesus to unleash all the power of His resurrection in our lives.

RIGHTEOUSNESS - Because of the resurrection, Jesus has the power to give us righteousness. This is the power of His resurrection. Jesus' crucifixion gives Him power over sin, so He can forgive, free and forget our sins. But it is Jesus' resurrection that gives Him the power to give us HIS righteousness by HIS power. Jesus not only helps us to stop doing what is wrong, but He also helps us to start doing what is right. Righteousness is not just not sinning, it is actually doing what is truly right and holy just like Jesus does.

This righteousness comes in three phases (Paul described this often in the book of Romans).

1. We were declared righteous when we came to Jesus and accepted Him as our Lord and Savior (justification is the theological word for that). That's when all our sins were forgiven because Jesus paid for them in full at the cross, and that's when all of Jesus' righteousness was credited to our account. Now God sees us as holy and righteous legally just as Jesus is. That's when we were born again into God's family, reconciled, and made at peace with God.
2. Now as followers of Jesus, Jesus lives in us to help us become actually as righteous as He is (sanctification is the theological word for that). He not only frees us from our sins, but He gives us the privilege now of doing what is right and holy and good just like He would do in any given situation of life. That is this amazing privilege of becoming conformed more and more to the image of Christ. We were created in the image of God, we lost that image in the fall, and now Jesus restores us to that image as He helps us to become more and more righteous and holy in the truth just like He is, just like we were created to be.
3. And the amazing hope is that someday when we get to heaven He will finish the work, so we will be perfected in His righteousness forever (glorification is the theological word for that). Not only will there be no more sin, but we will only think and act and talk and desire what is fully righteous all the time forever – just like Jesus does.

And it is this righteousness that leads us to life, God's life, eternal life, life to the full now and forever. We receive the gift of life when we are declared righteous. We enjoy the gift of life here on planet earth to the degree that we become righteous. We anticipate this perfected life in the presence of the Lord when we are completely righteous forever. Just as sin leads to death, so righteousness leads to life. Jesus died on the cross for our sins, so He can deliver us from sin and the judgment of death. And Jesus rose from the dead for our righteousness, so He can free us to rediscover His righteousness and receive and enjoy and anticipate this amazing gift of God's life to the full now in this lifetime and forever. Romans 5-6 describes how it is the power of the resurrection that enables Jesus to bring us His righteousness that gives us this amazing gift of life (Romans 5:21 – "grace reigns through righteousness to bring eternal life through Jesus Christ our Lord"). How awesome, amazing, priceless it is to get it right with Christ's righteousness the first time!

OBEDIENCE – We might wonder why then we still struggle with sin so much and why we find it so hard to find and live this righteousness and holiness and truth. Paul explains in Romans 6 that there is something we have to do as well. First we have to choose to believe the reality of our new life in Christ. We have to reckon, consider, account, count on these realities we have in Christ that we died with Christ to sin, and therefore we are dead to sin and have been freed from sin; and then that we were raised with Christ and therefore we live a new life unto God now in His righteousness (6:1-11). We can accept these truths upon the authority of God's Word. We can count on them, account them, consider and reckon them to be true. We choose to believe. We stake our life on them.

But then we have to choose whether or not to obey Jesus as Lord as He leads us into His righteousness. We were declared righteous when we chose to accept Jesus as our Lord and Savior. In the same way we become righteous when we choose to allow the risen Christ living in us to make us righteous and holy just like He is. Paul explained in Romans 6:12-16 that it is still our choice whether or not to let Jesus produce His righteousness in us. It is our choice whether or not we let sin reign as king/master or righteousness as king/master. It is our choice whether or not we let sin rule in our mortal bodies in this lifetime by obeying its lusts. It is our choice whether or not we present or offer our members as instruments (weapons) of unrighteousness to sin or to present ourselves to God and our members as instruments (weapons) of righteousness to God. But we must remember that to whom we present ourselves slaves unto obedience, we are slaves to whom we obey, whether of sin unto death or of obedience unto righteousness. We make the choice to obey Satan leading us to sin or to obey Jesus our risen Lord leading us to righteousness. The decision is totally ours.

It is exciting to realize that now we can actually become slaves to righteousness. When we came to Jesus, we chose the path of righteousness leading to life. In verses 17-23, Paul described how we chose to obey Jesus when we accepted Him as Lord/Savior. That is when we were set free from our slavery to sin and Satan, and we became slaves to righteousness. And just as we used to be slaves to sin leading to death, now we have become slaves to God and to His righteousness, leading to holiness and eternal life. The wages of sin are always death. But the gift of God is always righteousness leading to eternal life in Christ Jesus our Lord. Just as we used to be a slave to sin and free from righteousness, so now we have become slaves to righteousness who are free from sin. This doesn't mean we don't have a choice. We can still choose who is our master. But it does mean that when we choose to obey Jesus as Lord, when we choose to present/offer our members as instruments (weapons) of righteousness, we will just naturally do what is right. We will be slaves to righteousness and free from sin. We will just naturally become more and more like Jesus in righteousness and holiness in the truth. Just like we used to naturally live and talk and act in sinful, selfish ways, now we will supernaturally live and talk and act in righteous, loving ways. That is what happens when we truly seek first God's kingdom and His righteousness (Matthew 6:33).

Now it is unthinkable for us as Christians to continue in sin even though we are free to do so (Romans 6:1-2, 14-15). We can still choose to go back under sin and live under law if we want. God will not force us to walk in these new ways of grace leading to righteousness. We can still live in old ways of sin and unrighteousness and lawlessness, and they will always put us back as slaves to sin and Satan leading to corruption, destruction, death!!! Or we can choose to let Jesus give us the power to become righteous and live unto God for His kingdom, so that everything we do becomes an instrument or weapon for righteousness!! And to the degree we bow the knee before Jesus as Lord, we will find ourselves free to become more and more fully slaves of righteousness, who just supernaturally do what is right.

This is the power of Jesus living in us!! We can choose to let Jesus unleash in us all the power of His resurrection to make us truly holy and righteous with His very holiness and righteousness. That is when we begin to live life to the full – the life Jesus came to bring us!!

So the power is all of Jesus!! He died for our sins and conquered sin, Satan, death and hell, so that all our sins past, present and future can be fully forgiven, freed, forgotten now and forever. Jesus can deliver us fully from sin!! And then He rose from the dead to a new life that is forever, so that He can bring us into His kingdom where He is Lord and where He leads us into His righteousness giving us life to the full now here on the earth in this lifetime and in the new heaven and new earth for an eternity in the very presence of God forever. Jesus has all the power we would ever need to make us fully righteous and holy in the truth now and forever!!

The choice is totally ours – whether to accept His power or not!! Jesus has all the power He needs to transform every one of us. It doesn't matter how sinful we may be, how enslaved we may be, how deep our bondages may be, Jesus can not only free us from our sin but He can change us from the inside out to make us truly righteous and holy just like He is. But it is our choice to let Him do it as we simply obey Him as Lord of every area of our lives!!

Righteousness is how life was designed to be lived. Getting it right is so much better than getting it wrong. Righteousness leads to life to the full now and forever. Righteousness leads us to presenting our members, our time, our actions, our relationships, our work, our education, our entertainment, our everything as instruments to God for God to use to show off His glory and to build His kingdom. Righteousness leads to living unto God in everything.

By the power of the resurrection we can find a righteousness that is not our righteousness that we produce by trying to live up to God's law, but we find the righteousness of God, the righteousness that comes from Jesus Himself as He conforms us to His image in righteousness and holiness of the truth (see Philippians 3:7-11). It is not our job to change us on the inside and make us like Jesus. That is Jesus' job. He is the one who changes the way we think so we understand what is right, who works on our dreams and desires so we want what is right, and then who gives us the ability to do what is right (see Romans 12:1-2; Philippians 2:12-13). Our job is simply to obey, simply to present (offer/yield) ourselves to Jesus and His work in our lives, simply to choose to be slaves to righteousness and no longer slaves to sin. Whenever we choose to obey Jesus as Lord, Jesus unleashes His resurrection power and helps us do what is right. But whenever we refuse to obey Him, Jesus steps back and lets us make a mess and crash and bring pain and suffering and death and destruction until finally we become so miserable that we come back to Jesus and repent and confess and ask His forgiveness – and choose to obey Him again as Lord of all.

So if we want to get it right, including in these big things of life and marriage and family and most of all of our relationship with the God of heaven that determines life or death for this lifetime and an eternity, we have this confidence!! Jesus died for our sins, so all our sins can be forgiven, freed, and forgotten. And then Jesus rose from the dead for our righteousness, so we can be declared righteous, so we can become righteous, and ultimately so someday we can become perfected in righteousness forever. No wonder this message is called GOOD NEWS.

Here is a partial list of some of the things Jesus accomplished for us when He rose from the dead:

1. Christ was raised for our righteousness
   a. Jesus died for our sins and was raised for our righteousness – Romans 4:25.
   b. This includes justification as legal righteousness (Romans 3:20-24; 4:3, 22-25; 5:1, 15-21; 2 Corinthians 5:21) and sanctification as actual righteousness in our daily lives (Romans 6:4-23; 8:4, 10; 9:30-10:4; 10:5-13) and glorification as eternal righteousness (Romans 8:18-25; 1 Corinthians 1:8; 13:9-13; Philippians 1:6; 1 John 3:1-3).
   c. Righteousness is the true measure of success in our lives (Ephesians 1:4, 19-23; 4:11-16, 24: 5:9, 25-27; 1 John 2:29; 3:4-10).
   d. We should seek God's righteousness as the passion of our lives (Matthew 5:6; 6:33; Philippians 3:3-11).
   e. True righteousness will last for an eternity (1 Corinthians 3:11-15; Revelation 19:7-8).
   f. So the death of Christ delivers us from the power of sin, and His resurrection frees us to become holy and righteous.
2. Christ was raised to bring us into life to the full
   a. Jesus died to deliver us from death and was raised to bring us life. He came to give us the gift of eternal life (John 3:16, 36; 5:24; 10:10; 20:31 and many other places).
   b. This is first a spiritual life where we are born again into God's family and restored to a right relationship with Him (Ephesians 2:1-22). This life begins at the moment of salvation, grows to fullness in this lifetime, and lasts for an eternity. This is why the greatest essence of eternal life is knowing God the Father and Jesus Christ His Son (John 17:3).
   c. Then it is also a physical life with the hope that someday we will be raised again and given a glorified body just like Jesus has (John 5:28-29; Romans 8:18-23; 1 Corinthians

15:1-58; Philippians 3:20-21; 1 Thessalonians 4:13-18; Revelation 20:4-6). This confirms that physical pleasure is good (1 Timothy 4:1-5; 6:17; Revelation 21-22).
   d. So the death of Christ delivers us from the power of death and hell, and His resurrection frees us to enjoy eternal life now and forever – spiritually and physically.
3. The resurrection of Jesus teaches us how to focus on "the joy that is set before us" that enables us to endure the suffering and scorn the shame that come as we follow Jesus (Hebrews 12:2).
   a. The resurrection of Jesus leads us to great joy in the hope of God's ultimate victory (John 16:19-24; 1 Corinthians 15:12-58; 1 Peter 1:3-9).
   b. So as Christians living in Satan's world we face the persecution and suffering of life by fixing our eyes on Jesus (Hebrews 10:32-12:13).
   c. As we die to ourselves as followers of Jesus, it is the resurrection that gives us hope that God will exalt us in His time and His way. It is in dying with Christ that we find life in Him (Matthew 16:24-27; 19:16-30; Luke 14:26-33; 2 Corinthians 4:8-11; Philippians 3:3-11).
   d. So the death of Christ taught us to die to ourselves, and His resurrection frees us to live to Him in deep joy and hope.
4. The resurrection of Jesus leads us to a heaven-focused life rather than an earth-focused one.
   a. We seek the things above where Christ is (Colossians 3:1-4) rather than living according to human philosophies and teachings (Colossians 2:8, 16-23).
   b. We eagerly wait for our Savior rather than setting our minds on earthly things (Philippians 3:17-21).
   c. The hope of living forever with God in a new heaven and new earth motivates us to live now in the hope of eternal rewards (Romans 14:9-12; 1 Corinthians 3:11-15; 15:58; 2 Corinthians 5:10; 1 Peter 1:3-9; Matthew 6:19-24).
   d. This is the highest test of faith – are we willing to love Jesus more than anything else and truly present our lives to Him as living sacrifices (John 21:15-22; Romans 12:1-2)?
   e. So the death of Christ delivers us from living selfishly, and His resurrection frees us to live for Christ and His glory.

EXALTATION POWER
Chapter 6

Many people today don't believe Satan is real but that he is just something we have contrived to explain evil. But the Bible clearly speaks of a fallen angel called Satan who is very real and very much active in our world today. In fact, he deceives everyone in the entire world by his lies and lusts so they will reject God's truth and plan for their lives and will live instead for Satan and his kingdom (John 8:44).

That is why it is so exciting to understand that when we accept Jesus as our Lord and Savior, we are rescued from Satan's kingdom of darkness and death and introduced into God's kingdom of light and life by faith in Jesus Christ as God's Son (Colossians 1:12-14). And now Jesus has all the power we need to be delivered from all of the power of sin under Satan's control and to free us to live in all of God's righteousness under Jesus' control. That is the power of the death and resurrection of Jesus.

But no matter how far we are in this transformation process, we still all blow it and mess up. We are not perfect in this lifetime. We all have a long way to go. We still all give in to Satan's temptations to believe his lies and live for his desires. So what hope do we have that we can ever find the victory over Satan? Should we just give up and live in defeat and failure? Or can we find some path to freedom and victory and authority over Satan in our lives? I believe that it is the power of the exaltation of Jesus that gives us the hope and confidence that we can find victory and freedom over the power of Satan in our lives.

GOD GAVE JESUS ALL AUTHORITY. Jesus explained to His disciples after His resurrection that God had given Him all authority in heaven and earth (Matthew 28:18). And then He told them to lead people to become His followers (disciples) who will obey Him and His authority in everything (Matthew 28:19-20).

Forty days after God raised Jesus from the dead, He exalted His Son and seated Him at His right hand in heaven with all authority. In Ephesians 1:19-23 Paul said that the ultimate power of God was unleashed when He raised Jesus from the dead and exalted Him to heaven. That was the time when God gave Jesus all authority over all the powers of universe. God placed all things under the feet of Jesus and made Him head of all (see also 1 Corinthians 15:24-28). But for now this is a part of God's mystery that at this time He is still allowing people to choose whether or not to submit to Jesus as Lord (Ephesians 1:9-11). We as believers choose to do that today!!! But for unbelievers someday their knees will also bow and their tongues will also confess that Jesus is Lord (Philippians 2:9-11). But then it will be too late.

There is a sense in which Jesus has already totally defeated Satan and broken his power forever!! At the cross Jesus died for our sins, so now He can forgive, free, and forget all our sins and deliver us from death in all of its horrible forms. At the resurrection Jesus conquered death and rose to new life, so now He can lead us into His very righteousness leading to life to the full now and forever. At the exaltation Jesus was given all authority over Satan, so now He can lead us to find authority over Satan leading us to absolute victory over every aspect of Satan's control in our lives. This includes not only freedom from our sins but also from the consequences and ramifications of those sins. For example, in my own life I have found there are still many emotional and spiritual bondages from my legalism of the past, such as that law mindset that makes me still feel like a slave living in fear instead of like a son enjoying my Father's love (Romans 8:12-17). I am so excited to see that Jesus is working to free me from Satan's power in this and every area of my life.

In this mystery phase, God is still giving people the choice between Satan and Jesus. The reason is that God wants to give everyone time to repent and to choose to become His followers. God wants all to be saved and to come to the knowledge of the truth (1 Timothy 2:4). He is patient with us, not wanting anyone to perish but everyone to come to repentance (2 Peter 3:9). This means people can choose to leave Satan's kingdom of darkness and death and enter God's kingdom of light and life for this lifetime and forever. Or they can choose to stay. This also means that even we who have chosen to be followers of Jesus can still choose to believe and follow Satan's lies and lusts. Jesus has all authority in heaven and earth, but He leaves it up to us if we will choose to let Him unleash that power and authority in our lives.

God has given Jesus all authority in heaven and earth and seated Him at His right hand in the heavenly realms, far above all rule and authority, power and dominion, and every title that can be given not only in this present age but also in the one to come. And the mystery of God's will for this present age is that we are all free to choose to allow Jesus to bring every area of our lives into submission under His headship (Ephesians 1:20-21, 9-11). Jesus has all authority. But He leaves the choice up to us if we want to submit to that authority or not.

GOD GIVES US AUTHORITY TOO!! Paul prayed that we would know this power not only of the resurrection but also of the exaltation of Jesus (Ephesians 1:19-21). And as the body of believers (whole church), we are to demonstrate how great the power of Jesus really is to free us totally from Satan and to bring every area of our lives under His control (Ephesians 1:22-23). No one individual can show off all the fullness of Jesus' power. But each one of us can show off that portion of His power unleashed in our life. So male/female, young/old, rich/poor, educated/uneducated, religious/pagan, legalist/lawless all are a part of showing the greatness of the power of Jesus as our exalted

Savior and Lord by letting Him deliver us from the power of Satan in our lives and giving Jesus total control of every area of our lives.

Paul then explained that God has actually raised us up with Jesus and seated us with Him in the heavenlies (Ephesians 2:4-7). Just as we died with Christ and were raised with Christ, so we have been exalted with Christ. This means we share in His authority as we are seated with Him in the heavenlies. We do not have this authority on our own. But we have it in Christ, as we choose by faith to allow Him to take control and bring every area of our lives into submission and order under His control.

So we can look at Satan the way Jesus does – as a defeated enemy who has no right or power over us any longer. Satan had power over Jesus when Jesus was made to be sin for us. That's why Satan was able to unleash all the horror of spiritual and physical death on Jesus. But Jesus paid the price in full at the cross, rose triumphant, and now has all power and authority in heaven and earth including over Satan. And we do too!!

But we need to remember that we still all fail and stumble and are deceived so easily. We were totally messed up on the inside as sinners under Satan's power. Satan had total control of our mind and desires before we came to Jesus, so it takes a long time for us to let Jesus reprogram our thoughts, desires, actions, words. And our "default" mode is to listen to Satan's lies and live for his desires. So we still have a long way to go to get things totally right. Satan is a master deceiver. But we can win because we are now seated with Christ in the heavenlies!! And the more we believe and live that reality the more the victory we will experience.

Here's what Paul said we have to do to apply the power of Jesus in our daily lives (Ephesians 6:10-18). We have to be continually being strengthened in the Lord and His mighty power (three of same words used in Ephesians 1:19). We are totally dependent upon the Lord unleashing His power in us. We are constantly in a battle with supernatural, Satanic powers (verse 12). It is ridiculous to think we can ever win the battle in our own strength. But Jesus has all the supernatural power of heaven. He is God the Son who created the universe and then who died on a cross and rose again and is now seated at right hand of God with all authority in heaven and earth. And Jesus invites us to join Him in His victory and to use His supernatural power and His supernatural weapons formed by the power of His death and resurrection and exaltation, so we can crush Satan under our feet and stand victorious. We have to put on the whole armor that God gives us, which is simply the power that Jesus is unleashing in our lives. The armor of God is the power of the death, resurrection, exaltation of Jesus living in us (truth, righteousness, peace, faith, salvation, Word of God, praying always). When we do wear all this armor Jesus gives to us, we are able to stand in absolute victory no matter what Satan may throw at us.

So it's still our choice!! Jesus has all authority and power in heaven and earth, and He has everything we need for victory. He is constantly providing for us everything we need to walk in absolute victory. But Satan is still alive and well on planet earth, and he is unbelievably powerful and deceptive. He has unique strategies he is working in each of our lives. There may still be bondages and strongholds from the past that need broken. And there are always schemes he is masterminding to try to defeat us in the future.

But whenever we listen to Jesus and allow Him to work inside us, we will live in victory. No matter what Satan uses to try to deceive and destroy us, we will end up standing in victory. And Satan will crawl away in defeat. But whenever we don't listen to Jesus and don't allow Him to work inside of us, whenever we insist on doing things our way or in our power, whenever we listen to what other people may say or rely on how others may help us, we will end up under Satan's power and we will live in defeat.

That is why I ended up enslaved in legalism. I listened to what people said, the church said, my parents said, the religious leaders said. I thought I could do it if I just tried hard enough, and I was pleased with how good I was doing. But there was always a sense of failure, frustration, emptiness, and fear. But by the grace of God, He led me to believe what He said in His Word and then to choose to submit to Jesus and let Him change me on the inside by His power rather than by mine. As I look back over my life, all the times I have messed up have been because I tried to be strong in myself and to put on the armor that I built or that others built for me. But all the times I did what was right and holy in the truth have been because I came to Jesus as a messed up sinner and simply gave Him control of my life and chose to follow Him.

This is the path to victory: let the Lord strengthen us and give us everything we need to do it right. And then simply accept that strength and put on that armor and do it God's way by the power of Christ living in us. That is when Satan is powerless before us, and we end up standing in absolute victory!!

According to Ephesians 2:7, God wants us to live in our authority seated with Christ in the heavenlies for His eternal glory. Just think what that will be like for an eternity when God brags about us and what we allowed Jesus to do in our lives through the riches of His grace unleashed in the power of His death, resurrection, and exaltation. Like Paul described in Romans 6, we can offer the members of our bodies as instruments of sin to Satan to show off how horrible and messed up and painful and destructive sin really is. Or we can offer the members of our bodies as instruments of righteousness to God to show off how beautiful and wonderful and powerful and glorious Jesus really is – and the LIFE that He gives us. What a privilege to step into this authority we have in Christ for God's glory and ours – now in this lifetime and for the ages of eternity!! God wants to do immeasurably more than all we ask or imagine, according to His power that is at work within us, so that we can bring Him the glory throughout all generations, for ever and ever!" (Ephesians 3:19-20).

Jesus died for our sins to forgive, free, and forget all our sins forever, so that He can deliver us from death. Jesus rose for our righteousness to make us truly righteous and holy on the inside just like He is, so that He can give us life to the full now and forever. And Jesus was exalted to the right hand of God to give us authority over Satan, so that we can live in absolute victory over every aspect of Satan's power.

Jesus invites us to join Him in the excitement of knowing the battle is already fought and won. Yes, we live in a world that is still under Satan's power. And sometimes it seems like he is winning. But we have read the end of the Book, and we know God wins in the end – forever!! And so do all those who choose to be followers of Jesus as personal Lord and Savior. So for now we can live as more than conquerors because God always takes everything Satan does and works it together for good (Romans 8:28, 35-39). We are marching in triumph, with Satan dragging along behind as the defeated enemy (2 Corinthians 2:14-16). Even in the face of death, we have the ultimate victory even though Satan wins with the body for a short time (1 Corinthians 15:55-57). We can learn to say like Paul, "I can do everything through Him who gives me strength" (Philippians 4:13).

So no matter what we may face, no matter how Satan may attack us and threaten us and tempt us, we see ourselves seated with Christ in the heavenlies at the right hand of God with all authority in heaven and earth. Satan is a master-deceiver. He keeps screaming in our ears, "Loser … you're missing out … you'll never be free … everyone else is doing it … you can't help yourself ... Jesus is just one of many spiritual leaders ... you'll get it right if you just keep trying ...." But Jesus is whispering in our heart, "I love you, I died for you and your sins, I rose for your righteousness and your life, and I was exalted to the right hand of God with all power in heaven/earth." And then He tells us that we died with Him, were raised with Him and now are seated with Him. And we can live in all the power of His death, resurrection and exaltation if we will just trust Him and let HIM unleash in us all of His power.

It's our choice who we are going to believe and trust with our lives and our eternities!! But what we choose to do impacts the rest of our lives and the lives of those we love – for this lifetime and ultimately for an eternity.

Here is a partial list of some of the things Jesus accomplishes for us now that He is exalted to heaven:

1. Christ was exalted to have all authority in heaven and earth
    a. He announced this to His disciples (Matthew 28:18-20). This is focus of the great commission – leading others to be followers of Jesus who will always do whatever He commands.
    b. God the Father has given Jesus the authority to reign until He puts all His enemies under His feet. Then Jesus will present the entire universe to the Father (1 Corinthians 15:24-28).
    c. Jesus is often described as seated at the right hand of the Father in heaven until His enemies are His footstool (Matthew 22:44; 26:64; Acts 2:25, 33-34; 7:55-56; Romans 8:34; Ephesians 1:20; Colossians 3:1; Hebrews 1:3, 13; 8:1; 10:12; 12:2; 1 Peter 3:22).
    d. This is why the mystery of God's will is that we choose to give Jesus absolute authority in our lives as we submit to Him in everything (Ephesians 1:9-11, 19-23; 2:1-10; 5:22-33).

2. Christ was exalted to give us victory over Satan
   a. In His death and resurrection Jesus disarmed Satan and stripped him of his power by delivering us from law and forgiving us from sin (1 Corinthians 15:56-57; Colossians 2:15; Hebrews 2:14-15).
   b. Now Jesus is delivering us from Satan's power in our lives as we are strong in Him (Ephesians 6:10-18; 2 Corinthians 10:3-6).
   c. We are already exalted with Christ and seated with Him in the heavenlies with all of His power available to us (Ephesians 2:4-10; Philippians 3:20-21; Colossians 3:1-4; Hebrews 10:19-22).
   d. Satan is still working in our world today. Every time we give Jesus control of our lives, He is crushing Satan under His and our feet (Romans 16:20). Every time we choose sin, we give Satan control again (Romans 6:12-23).
   e. Now we can march in victory in the confidence that Christ is with us (Matthew 28:18-20; 2 Corinthians 2:14-16; 1 John 4:4).
3. Christ was exalted so He could send the Holy Spirit to us
   a. Jesus explained to His disciples that He had to go away for the Holy Spirit to come (John 16:5-7). And the Holy Spirit coming would be better than if Jesus would stay Himself.
   b. Peter explained on Pentecost that Jesus was exalted, so now He could pour out the Spirit (Acts 2:33-36).
   c. The purpose of the Spirit coming is so that we can hear and follow what Jesus is saying to us. This means Jesus can make His enemies a footstool for His feet by crushing Satan under our feet. And He does this through the Spirit bringing every area of our lives and ministries under the control of Jesus as Lord, thus giving us increasing victory over Satan.
   d. John explained that the Spirit could not be given until Jesus was glorified (John 7:37-39). But now that Jesus is glorified we who are thirsty can come and drink and be fully satisfied.
4. Christ was exalted to demonstrate He is Lord and Christ
   a. Peter explained on Pentecost that God has exalted Jesus to His right hand and made (declared) Jesus both Lord and

Christ (Acts 2:33-36). The resurrection publicly declared Him to be the Son of God (Romans 1:4); the exaltation publicly declared Him to be Lord and Christ.
b. After the death and resurrection of Jesus, God exalted Him to the highest place and gave Him the Name that is above every name – "Jesus Christ is Lord." And now the good pleasure of God that He is working in each of us is that we join Him in exalting His Son and truly letting Him be Lord in every area of our lives and ministries (Philippians 2:9-13).
c. We best show off the glory and power of Jesus as Lord as we allow Him to break Satan's power in our lives and bring us into complete victory and freedom in Him. It is as we experience all the power of the death, resurrection, and exaltation of Christ through the power of the Holy Spirit that we show off Jesus as Lord and the glory of His grace (Ephesians 1:6, 12, 14; 2:6-7; 3:10-11, 20-21). That is how we become the glorious, radiant church He is longing for us to be (Ephesians 5:25-27).

PART THREE

The Path to God's Mystery Power

FAITH WORKS
Chapter 7

I grew up understanding that I was saved at age seven when I received Jesus as my Lord and Savior by simple faith. But I assumed that after that point, I had to try hard to please God and become righteous by keeping a whole list of rules. I will never forget how at the age of 30 God got my attention while I was at the Cleveland Clinic for double-bypass open heart surgery (while my wife was getting ready to deliver our third child). He spoke to me very clearly from Romans 1:17 that "the just shall live by faith." That was a major turning point in my life as I finally realized that just as I was saved by faith, so now I must live and minister by faith. And that is the only way I can please God or become truly righteous.

Ever since that time I have been trying to figure out what faith is and how it works. I know that "faith is being sure of what we hope for and certain of what we do not see" (Hebrews 11:1). And I have been intrigued with the promise that if I have faith as small as a mustard seed, I can say to a mountain, "Move from here to there," and it will move, and nothing will be impossible to me (Matthew 17:20). And if I do not doubt in my heart but believe that what I say will happen, then it will be done for me (Mark 11:22-24). At the same time, I have concluded that these promises have been tragically abused by those who say that we will have health and wealth if we just believe that God will give them to us. And I have seen at times where I felt I was truly believing and not doubting – and God didn't give me what I was "believing" for.

So I continue to wrestle with the question of what faith is and how it works. But I really want to have the faith that God looks for and responds to. I have found that Hebrews 11 is probably the best place to go for God's answers to those questions. Here are a few conclusions I have reached from this passage.

True faith believes God is and God rewards. The faith that pleases God believes that God is and that He is Rewarder of those who earnestly seek Him (Hebrews 11:6). And without this faith it is impossible to please God – no matter how much we may try or sacrifice. Our faith is not in ourselves. And it's not in our faith. Our faith is in the person of God the Father and His Son Jesus and the Holy Spirit. We believe that God is and that God rewards those who seek Him. Faith is not some fuzzy feeling, some fantasy world we build and live in. Faith is always focused upon the Person of God and the reality of a living relationship with Him.

The whole chapter of Hebrews 11 illustrates that faith is always believing God and what He says and as an evidence of that faith simply obeying His commands and trusting His promises. By faith we believe that God is just as real as people around us. And we will stake our lives, our families, our careers, and our eternities upon Him and His promises. Abel, Noah, Abraham, Moses, and the others listed in Hebrews 11 all simply believed God and His Word – His promises, His commands, His power, His goodness, His eternal hope of heaven. And they obeyed. They believed when God intervened, and they believed when God did not. That is faith. And that is the faith that keeps us following God and trusting His promises and obeying His commands even when our world is falling apart and we seem to be losing everything, even our own lives.

We must remember that faith is never what moves God to do what we want but what moves us to do what God wants. Faith is always our response to God – not God's response to us. Faith always believes that God is and God rewards those who earnestly seek Him. All the men and women of faith listed in Hebrews 11 simply believed God and obeyed whatever He told them to do. Not a single one of them came up with their plan and demanded that God fulfill it just because they "believed." Instead they believed and obeyed God's plan for their lives even when that led to great suffering, sacrifice and sometimes even death. Jesus is the grand climax and ultimate example of what faith really is when He went to a cross to die for us in obedience to His Father's will for Him and in anticipation of God's reward (12:2-3).

True faith believes Jesus saves. And the heart of what God wants us to believe is His Son Jesus and what Jesus has accomplished for us in His death, His resurrection, and His exaltation. This is the message of the whole book of Hebrews and the entire Bible – Jesus is God's one and only plan to save us from our sins and give us this gift of eternal life. We are saved and live only by faith in Jesus as God's promised Messiah that He sent into the world to save us from our sins and give us life. This is the "command" that God gives us to believe – that Jesus is the Christ, the Son of the living God, and by faith we must accept Him and follow Him as our personal Lord and Savior. We are simply commanded to "fix our eyes of Jesus, the author and perfecter of our faith" (Hebrews 12:2, as conclusion of the faith of Hebrews 11).

This is also the message of the book of Romans – our faith is always in the person of Jesus. We know from Romans 1:17 that "the righteous will live by faith." According to Romans 1-8, we are saved by faith in Jesus, we live by faith in Jesus, and we die by faith in Jesus. By faith in Jesus we are declared righteous before God, by faith in Jesus we become righteous like God, and someday by faith in Jesus we will be glorified in perfected righteousness to be with God forever in heaven. And in Romans 9-11, Paul explains that God is sovereign. It doesn't matter how sincere we are, how much we want it, how hard we work for it, God has decided that He will only have mercy on those who believe in Jesus as God's Son and as their Lord and Savior!! Even God's chosen people who were trying to please God by keeping all the law missed out on God's blessings – because they didn't come to Jesus to put their faith in Him.

The entire Bible demonstrates that the focus of our faith is always on the person of Jesus as our Lord and Savior based upon what He has done and is doing and will do for us in His death, resurrection, and exaltation. In the Old Testament times, they looked forward to the coming Messiah and the hope of what God could do through Him to deal with their sin. In the New Testament times, they talked and wrote about why Jesus came and how this new covenant of grace works – totally by faith in Jesus and what He accomplished for us in His death, His resurrection, and His exaltation.

Faith in Jesus is the greatest, most important focus of our faith – and what God wants more than anything else. This is what brings God His greatest pleasure and what brings us our greatest blessing – living by faith in Jesus. Faith is always rooted in a personal relationship with the God of heaven, believing He is and He rewards those who come by faith to His Son Jesus to accept Him and follow Him as Lord and Savior of every part of their lives as long as they live. True faith believes Jesus saves and comes to Him to let Him save us!!

True faith works. Faith is more than just believing in God as some abstract theological truth. In Hebrews 11, all the men and women of faith were called to obey and follow God, often in face of great opposition and suffering from the world around them. Faith is not just some abstract philosophical concept – it is radical obedience to God and His will, believing God is and God rewards. James 2:14-26 reinforces this truth. Faith is more than believing facts about God. The demons believe the facts, and they tremble. True faith always leads us to obey. True faith works. And any faith that does not work, that does not obey God, is a dead faith – not a real faith at all.

Of course, the Bible is clear that we are saved by faith and not by works – and we live that way too. We do not earn or deserve God's grace in our lives by our works because then we would take the glory to ourselves instead of giving it all to God (Ephesians 2:8-9). But at the same time God has good works prepared in advance that we should walk in them (Ephesians 2:10). And from the context the primary focus of those good works is showing off what God in His grace can do in and through us by the power of Jesus saving us and living in us (Ephesians 2:1-7). He can deliver us from the bondage of sin, Satan, death and hell in every area of our lives. He can make us alive in Christ and actually seat us with Him in the heavenlies with all authority over Satan and Satan's power in our lives. He can pour out the exceeding riches of His grace in His kindness to us in ways that He can point to for an eternity to demonstrate His glory. That's amazing grace – that we get to live to the praise of the glory of His grace now and forever (Ephesians 1:6, 12, 14; 2:7; 3:20-21). These are the true works of faith, following Jesus as Lord as He unleashes in us all the power of His death, His resurrection, and His exaltation.

Faith is simply submitting to God's will as He works in us to will and to do of His good pleasure which is that we exalt His Son Jesus by bowing our knee and confessing with our mouth that Jesus is Lord (Philippians 2:9-13). This is living by the faith that brings God His greatest glory and His greatest pleasure. And this is how we find God's greatest reward and greatest blessing in our lives, bringing us our greatest pleasure now and for an eternity. This is what God wants for us to do more than anything else – to join Him in His supreme pleasure of glorifying and exalting His Son Jesus as Lord of all. This is what He is working in us to will and to do, and true faith will simply "work out" what God is "working in" us.

This is the ultimate way that faith works – letting Jesus unleash in and through us all the power of His death, His resurrection, and

His exaltation. We believe that Jesus is who He says He is and that He can do what He says He can do. We believe that the power is all of Jesus. Faith simply chooses to accept the power He provides and to live in that power. Whatever Jesus provides for us each day, we accept it and live by it. Whatever Jesus leads us to do and think and say and be, we do, think, say, and be by His power. This is the reality of Colossians 1:27, "Christ in us the hope of glory." That is the true faith that works.

True faith is in God alone. When we read the OT, we see the Jewish people breaking God's heart over and over again because they put their faith in some foreign government to protect and provide for them – Egypt, Syria, Babylon, etc. And worse yet, they put their faith in and worshiped the gods and goddesses of the nations around them rather than Yahweh. That is why God judged them so severely by allowing foreign nations to conquer and take them captive. That is why we must be so careful where we are putting our faith today for the eternal, spiritual realities of life. There is the danger of putting our faith in the gods of education, of Hollywood, of our family and friends, of the latest psychological or scientific studies, of the latest talk-show host, of the latest author, or of our government. And there is the danger even of putting our faith in our church, our denomination, our pastors and elders, the latest Christian author or singer or performer, the latest set of Christian rules and regulations, or our church's theology and traditions. And there is the danger of putting our faith in ourselves – our abilities to figure things out, what makes sense to us, what brings us the greatest pleasure, what brings us the greatest praise from others. And wherever we put our faith, we end up obeying what these "gods" demand.

God is looking for people who will dare to believe that He is God and that He rewards those who earnestly seek Him. And we seek Him by coming to Jesus and living by faith in Him, as we bow in humble obedience to Jesus as Lord in every area of our lives. God is looking for people with a true faith, a true faith that works – that simply works out what God is working in, that simply lives out all the power that Jesus has provided for us in His death, resurrection, and exaltation. These people bring God pleasure.

What God wants more than anything else is that we bow the knee and confess with our mouth and our lives that Jesus Christ is Lord!!!! That means we will seek to obey Him always in everything!!! And upon these people God pours out His rewards – in His time and in His way. Sometimes that is in this lifetime, sometimes it is not until we get to heaven. Sometimes it is just in the spiritual realm, sometimes it is also in the physical realm. Sometimes we see it, sometimes we don't for now. But faith dares to believe that God is and that God rewards those who earnestly seek Him in His time and in His way.

This is the mustard-seed faith that can move mountains. This is the faith that looks at whatever God tells us He wants us to do and believes with confidence that God will give us everything we need to do it. Where we see sin and death and those Satanic patterns that have become our way of life, we can by faith move those mountains by the power of the death of Christ. Where we look at God's righteousness and His life that seem so impossible to attain, we can by faith move those mountains by the power of the resurrection of Christ living in us. Where we look at the bondages and the strongholds that Satan has built in our lives, we can by faith move those mountains by the power of the exaltation of Christ living in us. When we believe in God and come to Jesus by faith and faith alone and hear what Jesus is saying to us as His will and plan for us, we can by faith move those mountains and have the very things we have asked of God. That is when we can do the impossible – because Christ is living in us. That is when we can live in the reality of Philippians 4:13: "I can do everything through Him who gives me strength" – when we seek to do the things that Jesus is giving us His strength to do!!

In fact, this is when we can do even greater works than Jesus did when He was on the earth (John 14:12-14). Jesus lived and ministered under the Old Testament law system with all of its weakness and imperfections. We live under the New Testament grace system with all the reality and power of Jesus' death, resurrection, and exaltation. That is why the works we do are even greater works than what Jesus could do. These are not works we do in our power. These are not good works we do to earn God's grace. These are actually the works of Jesus Himself, living and working in us and through us in all the power of His death, resurrection and exaltation. As we live by faith, we are able to do whatever Jesus gives us to do by His power and for His glory.

True faith simply bows before Jesus as Lord and gives Him absolute control in our lives. True faith believes that whatever Jesus wants to do in and through us, He can do. And true faith lets Him do it through all the power of His death, His resurrection, and His exaltation. This is the faith that truly pleases God, the faith that truly believes that God is and God rewards.

GRACE LIBERATES
Chapter 8

As I think of where the Lord has most radically changed my life, I believe it is in how He has led me out of the deception of living under law to the freedom of living under grace. He led me first to a Biblical conviction and then to applying that grace in my family, my ministry, and hardest of all in myself. And after all these years, there are areas of my life where I am still struggling to let Jesus lead me to live completely under grace.

I have come to believe that living under law may be one of Satan's most deadly strategies and possibly the one he uses more than any other. This can take two forms – rebelling against God's law or trying our hardest to please God by living under His law. Most people will fall into one trap or the other, and they often bounce back and forth between these two deceptions. Satan knows that as long as he can keep us living under law, Jesus will not be able to work in our lives in the power of grace. In Galatians 5:1-4, Paul wrote that if we live under law, Christ will be of no value to us at all, we will be obligated to obey the whole law, we have been alienated from Christ, and we have fallen from grace. No wonder it has been and still is possibly the most deadly strategy Satan has to keep us from Jesus and all that He wants to do in our lives.

I have found that the book of Romans has helped me as much as anywhere else in the New Testament to learn how faith and grace are tied together so much in contrast to works and law. We are saved by faith in God's grace, we live by faith in God's grace, we minister by faith in God's grace, and we die by faith in God's grace. Just as we are saved and live only by faith not works, so we are saved and live only under grace not law.

Grace is what God gives us. We need to understand that grace is simply a gift that God gives us. This is the meaning of the word. God graciously or freely gives us something that we don't deserve. We cannot work for it or earn it or deserve it because then it would be wages God owes us. Instead God gives it to us as a gift. And faith simply reaches out to receive the gift.

Grace is totally what God does for us, not what we do for God. When we live under law, we see a whole list of things we do for God. But when we live under grace, we see a whole list of things God does for us. We realize that our salvation from start to finish is totally all of God and His grace for us. We accept that we are saved by faith in God's grace and not by works trying to live up to God's law. And we accept that we live by that same faith in that same grace!!

The New Covenant of Grace has now replaced God's Old Covenant of Law as the way we approach God and live for His pleasure. The purpose of law was to show us how sinful we are and how much we need a Savior (Romans 3:19-20; Galatians 3:21-25). But now that Jesus has come to be our Savior, we no longer are under the law but under grace (Romans 6:14-15; Galatians 3:23-25). Notice that even God's perfect law could never free us from the power of sin (Romans 6:14). Paul explained in Romans 7 that actually law is what gives sin its power, something for sin to rebel against. And no matter how hard we try to live up to God's law, we will keep failing over and over again. And if God's perfect law cannot free us from sin, how much less will man-made rules and regulations ever do so. In contrast, God's grace not only frees us from sin but it also frees us to live in righteousness, where we will just naturally want to do what is right and good (Romans 6:14-23).

Grace does what law could never do – it changes us on the inside to help us become like Christ. Grace enables us now actually to fulfill the law and please God. In Romans 8:1-8 we see that those living under law cannot keep the law and cannot please God. But those living under grace fulfill the law and please God by becoming holy and righteous like God is. So grace does not ignore God's moral absolutes, instead it empowers us actually to live up to those standards of holiness and righteousness in the truth. Grace enables us to keep the law and please God, because the righteous requirements of the law are actually fully met in us (Romans 8:4).

Grace is simply everything that God has made available to us now through the power of Jesus alive and living in us. Jesus died on a cross as a sacrifice in our place to deliver us from sin and death. Jesus rose from the grave as the firstborn of a new creation to free us for righteousness and life. Jesus was exalted to heaven with all authority in heaven and earth to give us all authority over Satan so we can live in complete victory over Satan and his power in our lives. So living under grace is simply coming to Jesus by faith, a faith that works, a faith that lets Jesus work in our lives however He wants not only to deliver us from the power of sin, Satan, death, and hell but also to free us now to enjoy life to the full in holiness and righteousness and truth. All we do to accept this gift of grace is to come by faith to submit to Jesus as Lord and give Him absolute control in our lives.

Grace is God's gift to us. But we are free to choose whether or not to accept and live that gift. Satan tries to get us to live under law because law keeps us defeated and living under Satan's control. Grace frees us from Satan's control and makes us super-conquerors in Christ. That's why God desperately begs us to live under grace by faith in Jesus and what He can do in and through us. Our faith must be in Christ and Christ alone as He lives in us to save us and set us free to become like Him. One of the most important decisions of our Christian lives is to choose to live under grace and not under law.

Grace brings us into God's love. I am so thankful for all the Lord has taught me over the years about this gift of grace and what it means to live under grace and not under law. And I know I still have a lot more to learn. The Lord has taught me much about the theology of grace. He has taught me much about building my marriage upon grace, about parenting under grace, about ministering under grace. But I have had the hardest time letting Him teach me to apply that grace to my own life and relationship with Him. In recent years the Spirit has used Romans 8:14-17 many times to show me the remnants of that law mindset in my life that are still robbing me of so much that my Father wants me to enjoy.

After Paul carefully explained grace in Romans 1-8, he described the huge difference between how we relate with God under law compared to how we relate with God under grace (8:14-17). When we still live under law, we approach God as slaves trembling in fear. But when we live under grace, we come boldly before God as His sons and daughters, calling out with joy and excitement, "Abba, Father." And we live in the delight of knowing we are heirs of God and co-heirs with Jesus of all the riches of God's universe. God wants us to live as sons and as heirs of God. God wants us to relax in His presence as His children, not trembling in fear as slaves.

Law gives us a spirit (an inner attitude) of living as a slave in fear before a master who owns us and demands our obedience. We live in constant fear, guilt, and condemnation every time we mess up. And the harder we try to get it right, the more we mess up and are crushed with more fear, guilt, and condemnation. That is the purpose of the law – to show us how sinful and guilty we really are (Romans 3:19-20). This may drive us to try harder and harder to try to get it right in the hopes that someday maybe we can please our Master or it may lead us to give up in despair and decide to run away and do our own thing. Either way we always end up saying with Paul, "What a wretched man I am! Who will deliver me from this body of death" (Rom 7:24).

But grace gives us a spirit of sonship and teaches us to look at God as our Father and to cry out, "Abba, Father." "Abba" was the family term of children loving and relaxing with their daddy. There is still a sense of reverent fear and respect for our Heavenly Father. But now we serve our Father because we know He loves us and we love Him. There is now no longer this feeling of fear, guilt, condemnation (Romans 8:1). Instead, now we see ourselves as heirs of all the riches of God's grace, of all the spiritual blessings of the heavenlies (Ephesians 2:7; 1:3). We are heirs of God and co-heirs with Jesus. We are God's family. And since we are serving in the family business, now our hard work not only builds our Father's business but it also increases our riches as well. We are no longer working for a paycheck never knowing when we will get fired or executed for doing a bad job. Now we are working as a son or daughter for our inheritance in the family business, knowing we are secure in God's love. It has already been decided that we are sharing in the benefits of the business forever. And Romans 8:28-39 concludes with this amazing truth that not only does God work all things together for good, but also nothing in the entire universe can ever separate us from God and His love for us that we have in Christ Jesus our Lord. Now rather than living in fear, we are living in the absolute confidence of our security in God's love now and forever!!

So what do we need to do to learn to relax as a son instead of living in fear as a slave? Part of learning to relax is realizing we can't find some "law" to obey that will fix our problem. It's not a list of rules we have to keep or ways we have to try harder and harder. Instead we need to let the Holy Spirit teach us to call out "Abba, Father" and to relax and live under our Father's love. We need to let God transform us by the renewing of our minds and by working in us to will and to do of His good pleasure. Our job is simply just to respond by the faith that dares to believe what God says and no longer to believe the lies that Satan keeps feeding us. So when we have thoughts and feelings of fear or when we try to come up with some list of rules we need to keep, we can identify those as deceptions from Satan. But as we have thoughts and feelings affirming how much God loves us and making us want to relax with our Father, with Jesus, and with the Spirit, then we can know that is the work of the Holy Spirit in us teaching us to call out "Abba, Father" as His son or daughter and as His heir forever.

So it is our choice!! And that choice should be a no-brainer. We can live as slaves in fear, never knowing when we have done enough to please our master. Or we can live as sons or daughters and heirs, always knowing we are secure forever in our Father's love because we believe that Jesus has done enough!!

My wife and I love being with our children and grandchildren, and we love being with extended family and friends. But we really, really love just being together and relaxing together in our love for one another. The thing I want the most from my wife and the thing she wants the most from me and the thing that we want the most from our kids and our grandkids is this amazing thing called love. And Jesus explained that what God wants from us more than anything else is our love (Matthew 22:37-40). God created us in His image to be able to relax together as His family in love, where we enjoy His love and He enjoys our love. Sin destroys that. And Law distorts that by making us slaves under fear. But grace restores that by forgiving our sin and freeing us from fear and making us sons or daughters of God who can relax in God's love and cry out "Abba, Father!!" Grace liberates us to be able to love God again with all our heart, soul, mind and strength the way He created us and now redeemed us to be able to love.

God is inviting us, begging us to come home and relax in His love. He longs for us to come home and learn to laugh and play and tell

God how much we love Him. He longs for us to come home by faith in Jesus and learn to live under grace and not under law. He longs for us to dare to believe that we are sons and daughters of God and not slaves living in fear. That is when we can get excited about working in the family business, knowing we have this amazing privilege of working side by side with the God we love in the business that is bringing Him glory and us pleasure for this lifetime and forever.

So let's choose grace!! And let's allow grace to liberate us to enjoy life as sons and daughters of the God of heaven who loves us with a perfect love and who invites us to learn to love Him with that same love as His family now and forever!! That is when we can relax in the ultimate joy of being truly home with the love of our lives, knowing that His love and our love will last forever!!

SPIRIT ENERGIZES
Chapter 9

As I look back over how the Lord has been radically changing me, I see how He has been teaching me that I must live by faith and not by works and that I must live under grace and not under law. That is the only way I can experience the power and reality of Christ living and working in me in all the power of His death, His resurrection, and His exaltation. But I also see how He has been teaching me that I can only experience this power as I live in the power of the Holy Spirit and not in the power of my flesh. This seems to be the area that God has been dealing me with in particular in these recent years.

The night before Jesus went to the cross, He explained to His disciples that He was going to send the Holy Spirit to live in them and to guide them into all truth. And He said that this would even be a better plan than if He Himself would stay with them (John 14:16-17, 26; 15:26-27; 16:7-15). Then after His resurrection Jesus gave them the promise, "You will receive power when the Holy Spirit comes on you; and you will be My witnesses in Jerusalem, and in all Judea and Samaria, and to the ends of the earth" (Acts 1:8). And of course, that has been fulfilled for all who believe in Jesus as their Lord and Savior, beginning on the Day of Pentecost down to today (Acts 2:38-39).

We must walk in the Spirit and not in the flesh. This is a choice we all must continually make. Just as we must choose to live by faith and not by works and to live under grace and not under law, so we must choose to walk in the Spirit and not in the flesh (NIV translates as "sinful nature"). Paul talked about how radically different life in the flesh is from life in the Spirit in Romans 7-8 and in Galatians 5-6. In both places Paul explained very clearly about how we must live by faith in God's grace not by works of law. So I believe these three things all tie together: either we live by faith in God's grace through the power of the Spirit or we live by works of law in power of the flesh.

Flesh is simply me, my power, my efforts, my struggles, me doing what makes sense to me. In Romans 7:18 Paul wrote that nothing good dwells in us, that is in our flesh. He goes on to describe the flesh as his attempts to please God by keeping God's law but totally failing. No matter how hard we try we can never keep the law. Instead we keep doing what we don't want to do and not doing what we want to do. The reason is that no matter how much we may want to keep the law, when we try to keep the law in the efforts of the flesh, we end up setting our minds on the things of the flesh. And the flesh leads to death, the flesh is hostile to God, the flesh does not submit to God's law nor can it, and those controlled by the flesh cannot please God (Romans 8:5-8). In Galatians 5:16-26, Paul explained that walking in the flesh will always lead us in ways that are opposite to walking in the Spirit. There Paul listed some of the horrible things that will characterize the lives of those walking in the flesh (see verses 19-21). These are not what flesh is. Instead these are the works of the flesh or the result of living life in our power, doing what makes sense to us. In contrast, when we are walking in the Spirit and not in the flesh, our lives will be characterized by the fruit of the Spirit, as the supernatural result of the Spirit controlling our lives (see verses 22-24). And what a difference this makes!! Paul made it clear in Galatians 6:7-8 that whenever we walk in the flesh, the flesh will always produce a harvest of destruction and death. But whenever we walk in the Spirit, the Spirit will always produce a harvest of life now and forever!!

So from my understanding, walking in the flesh is simply doing my thing, in my ability, in ways that make sense to me. That may lead me to live in blatant rebellion against God and His law, or that may lead me to try my hardest to please God and keep His law. In contrast, walking in the Spirit is simply giving the Holy Spirit control in my life as He leads me to submit to Jesus as Lord in every area of my life.

My life verse has been Philippians 3:10-11, "I want to know Christ and the power of His resurrection and the fellowship of sharing in His suffering, becoming like Him in His death, and so, somehow, to attain to [the power of] the resurrection from the dead [now and forever]." But I have found that the only way I can experience that reality is when I "put no confidence in the flesh" but put all confidence in Christ and Christ alone. And the way that Paul illustrated "flesh" is that he talked about his heritage, his education, his righteousness according to the law, his zeal. Before he met Christ, he was sure he was pleasing God because of all these things he was doing. But once he met Jesus, all these things he had accomplished seemed like so much manure or rubbish in comparison to what he was finding in Jesus. And instead of treasuring the manure, he wanted to live the rest of his life seeking to know Jesus and all the righteousness and resurrection power he could experience in Jesus.

So we must face the reality that there are two ways to live our lives – in the flesh (our power) or in the Spirit (God's power). The only way we can ever live by faith in all the riches of God's grace is as we walk in the power of God's Holy Spirit. Whenever we try to please God by our works of law in the power of the flesh, we end up in frustration, failure, and death. Our righteousness and accomplishments that we achieve in the efforts of the flesh are always manure or rubbish to us and filthy rags to God (Philippians 3:8; Isaiah 64:6). And they will all be burned up in the fire at the judgment seat of Christ as so much wood, hay, straw (1 Corinthians 3:12-15). But when we choose to please God by faith in His grace through the power of the Spirit, that is when we find the freedom as sons to live in the very righteousness of God that truly pleases God and us. Paul explained that because of the work of Jesus "the righteous requirements of the law are fully met in us, who do not live according to the flesh but according to the Spirit" (Romans 8:4).

<u>Spirit Power makes us living witnesses of Jesus.</u> This is simply what Jesus promised before He went back to heaven, "You will receive power when the Holy Spirit comes on you; and you will be My witnesses" (Acts 1:8). A witness is simply someone who tells others what he has seen or heard or experienced. I am a witness who can tell you what it is like to have open-heart bypass surgery, not because I read about it in a book but because I experienced it in real life. The followers of Jesus were to go out into the world as witnesses of the fact that Jesus Christ had died for their sins and risen from the dead and was exalted to heaven at the right hand of God and that He is truly the Son of God who saves and gives eternal life to all who believe in Him. They were to be witnesses of the fact that Jesus was alive and living and working in them, changing their lives and setting them free from sin, Satan, death and hell so now they could live a whole new life pleasing to God in all holiness, righteousness and truth.

And that is simply what the early believers did. They simply talked about Jesus and His life, death, resurrection, and exaltation and the fact that now God offers salvation to any who believe in Him. They were very conscious of the fact that they were witnesses of these things (see Acts 2:32; 3:15; 4:18-20, 29-31, 33; 8:4-5, 35; 10:39-43; 13:30-31). Now we are to be witnesses of the fact that Jesus is still alive today and living and working in our lives today. We have not seen Jesus dying on the cross nor appearing to us after His resurrection. But we can experience Him alive and living in us. And we can tell the world that He is alive because we see Him living in us and saving us and radically changing our lives. God wants us to be dynamite witnesses of the awesome realities we are experiencing in our daily lives not just robots reciting some theological facts we have read in a book somewhere.

And we desperately need the Spirit's power to be able to be such witnesses of Jesus (Acts 1:4-5). Jesus told His disciples to wait until they received the Holy Spirit. They were not ready even though they had seen Jesus in His resurrection body and even though Jesus Himself had explained the Old Testament Scriptures to them (Luke 24:45-49). How much more must we need the Spirit's power to be witnesses of Jesus today!! We are handling the truths of the greatest reality of all of human history – God offers a salvation that delivers us from eternal death and gives us eternal life!! This is the eternal plan of God the Father and the work of God the Son delivered through God the Holy Spirit. And we are invading Satan's kingdom of darkness and death to rescue people from his power and bring them into God's kingdom of light and life. That is why Jesus told them and us to wait until we are filled with the Holy Spirit and given His power – even though we may know all the theological facts of the Gospel.

It is exciting to see that God promised in these last days to pour out His Spirit upon all flesh (Acts 2:16-21). At the day of Pentecost, God gave a unique gift to validate His followers and their message – an ability to speak in other languages so that people from all different countries could hear about Jesus in their own heart language. When some accused them of being drunk, Peter said that they were simply experiencing what God had promised in Joel 2:28-32. Previous to this time, God sent His Holy Spirit upon just a select group of people and often just for a period of time or for a special assignment – a priest, a king, a prophet. Jesus was filled with the Holy Spirit for those years of His public ministry. But now God was going to pour out His Spirit upon all people who are believers, male and female, young and old. Notice the significance of this. Men as well as women – equally empowered. Young as well as old – equally empowered. Those were radical thoughts in the society of that day. The power of the Holy Spirit is just as real for each believer on that Day of Pentecost and yet today. We don't have to be a preacher, an elder, a deacon or deaconess. We just have to be a believer. This gift of the Holy Spirit is for any who put their faith in Jesus Christ as personal Lord and Savior (Acts 2:38-39).

And the primary result of God giving the Spirit is that they would prophesy. The heart of the word "prophesy" is to "speak for God." We will speak the very words that God gives us to speak. And when we connect this back to what Jesus said would be the result of the Holy Spirit being poured out upon us as believers, possibly this prophesying means primarily that we will receive power to be living witnesses of Jesus (Acts 1:8). I have been intrigued with what the angel said to John as Jesus was revealing to him God's future plans, "For the testimony ("witness," the same word as in Acts 1:8) of Jesus is the spirit of prophecy" (Revelation 19:10). This "testimony of Jesus" may be the "prophesying" that all of us as believers are to be doing. We are not prophets with the gift of prophecy receiving new revelation from God that is to be recorded in inspired Scripture. But we are prophesying or speaking words God gives us to speak when by the power of the Spirit we are living witnesses of Jesus. We are prophesying or being witnesses of Jesus when we are showing the power of what Jesus Christ can do in our lives through the power of His death setting us free from sin, the power of His resurrection setting us free for righteousness, and the power of His exaltation setting us free for victory over any areas of Satanic bondage in our lives.

The more we are filled by the Holy Spirit and experiencing the power of the Holy Spirit, the more clearly and boldly we will be living witnesses telling others that Jesus Christ is alive and living and working in us as we show and tell what He is doing in our lives. And we can tell those we are talking to the good news that they can experience that same reality in their lives as well, if they too will come by faith to accept Jesus as their personal Lord and Savior.

<u>We can be filled with this Spirit power</u>. This Spirit power is available for every one of us as believers. But to experience this Spirit power in our lives, we have to learn how to quit living and walking in the flesh and begin living and walking in the Spirit.

This means we have to let go of the control of our own lives and also of the lives of others. We have to believe that the Holy Spirit fills young and old alike, rich and poor alike, conservative and liberal alike, modern and post-modern alike, Boomers and Gen-Xers and Millennials alike. Think about the early church. They started as 120 Jewish believers in an upper room. They could all fit comfortably. They all knew one another's names. They all continued in one accord (Acts 1:14). Then there were 3,000 saved and added to church in one day, and they still continued in one accord (2:46). At least they were all Jews who now had decided to follow Jesus. But then Samaritans were saved, then Gentiles, then the radical persecutor Saul, and then the church spread around the Roman Empire. There were slaves and masters, male and female, Jew and Greek, sophisticated and barbarian. The early believers had to "let go" of their control and let Jesus build His church however He decided. In the same way today we have to "let go." We have to trust God to be God. And we have to let Jesus Christ build His church in His time and in His way through the power of the Holy Spirit. It is not our church. It never has been and it never will be. It is His church. He bought it and He builds it! God wants a people who will let go of all their rights, their control, their plans and let God be God!! It is not the pastor's way, the elders' way, the deacons' way; it is God's way!! And of course, God also wants us to let go personally of our rights, dreams, and ambitions and give Him control of every area of our lives. That is when the Holy Spirit can fill us with His power to be and do all that Jesus wants us to be and do.

This also means we have to choose to let the Spirit fill us and work in and through us however He wants. Tragically we have been so afraid of the Holy Spirit in most evangelical churches that we have developed patterns of life and ministry that are simply our efforts, our works, our flesh. Nothing really exciting happens because we are simply doing the same things over and over again. This is what I have seen as one of biggest battles of my life and ministry and in evangelical church today. So I am talking about me and the church I know and love. God in His grace has been working so patiently in my life to deliver me from this confidence in the flesh and to help me to find and minister in Spirit power. More and more I long for life and ministry totally in the power of the Holy Spirit filling, controlling and empowering me to be a living witness of Jesus alive and living in me. And I long to see others living in that same Spirit power.

I long for Christ to build His church today in such a way that there is no explanation but God. But for that to happen we have to let go of the flesh totally, of any confidence in ourselves and our wisdom and abilities and hard work. We have to let go of all our control and let God the Holy Spirit take full control of our lives and ministries and use us however He pleases!! And we also have to let go in our individual churches. We cannot hang on to things the way they have always been. We cannot live based on what we think, what we want, what we can do. We cannot hide in the shadows any longer thinking we are too weak, too small, too shy, too old!!

We must dare to believe that God the Holy Spirit has moved into each one of our lives as believers, and He has brought with Him all the power of the death, resurrection, and exaltation of Jesus. He can change our lives miraculously. And He can use us miraculously however He desires!! But we must each one do this personally. The only way our families or our churches will change is as we as individuals dare to change and allow Spirit to work in us!! He is just waiting for us to let go of our control and let Him take over!!

Then we can be living witnesses of Jesus alive and living in us. Young and old. Male and female. When we give Jesus control, we will simply have one thing we want to do, one thing we want to talk about, one thing we are excited about, one thing we want to build our church around – JESUS!! We will simply be living witnesses of Jesus. And we will see that the only thing that matters as a church is being living witnesses of Jesus – to one another as family and to a lost world around us. We will simply want to live lives that are being constantly changed and radically transformed, so that we can show off more and more the power and reality of Christ living in us. We will simply preach Jesus Christ, and Him crucified, risen, exalted!! That is what Paul concluded was His entire ministry to unbelievers and believers alike (1 Corinthians 1-2). We can dare to believe that when Christ is lifted up, that is when He will draw all people to Himself (John 12:32). There is even an intriguing statement in 1 Corinthians 14:24-25 that when an unbeliever or untrained person comes in to a church and all are prophesying (talking about Jesus), that person will be convicted by all and will fall down and worship God!! It's not the sound of our music, the creativity of our preaching that will bring people back to God. It's Jesus!!

God is simply looking for people who will join Him in exalting His Son Jesus (Philippians 2:9-13). That is what God wants, that is what the Spirit wants, and that is where Jesus will work!! God longs for His family to grow. Think of the awesome price that God has paid to save people in our communities and around the world. And think of all that Jesus has done over the years in saving us and changing us and helping us. God is simply looking for individuals, families, groups of believers who are willing to join Him in the greatest mission in all the world!! God invites us right now to let go of our control, to be filled with the Spirit, and to become vibrant living witnesses of Jesus through the power of the Holy Spirit. God invites us to be the people who will show the church and show the world one more time that Jesus is truly alive and living in us – and that He can save and change anyone who comes to believe in Him and accept and follow Him as Lord and Savior of every area of their lives!!

PART FOUR

The Delights of God's Mystery Power

MAKING LOVE WITH JESUS
Chapter 10

God has blessed me with an amazing wife for almost fifty years. Our greatest joy in marriage has been learning to be one together – no longer two. This oneness is the real goal and pleasure of marriage – where we live together as one in love and harmony mentally, socially, emotionally and most of all spiritually. But we have also really, really enjoyed the celebration of that oneness where we become one physically as well in this amazing gift of sex that God has given to us.

Over the years of marriage, I have come to believe that my relationship with my wife is just a little picture of the relationship that God wants to have with me and that God wants me to have with Him. And it has been an exciting adventure to ask God to teach me what that really means and how to live that out in my daily walk with Him.

Let me first share some Biblical perspectives that have helped me reach that conclusion. In the beginning God created Adam in God's own image. And then once Adam realized what God knew that Adam needed "a helper suitable for him," God created a woman for him. And God performed that first wedding ceremony and told them to enjoy sex and have lots of children. And God declared His creation of love and marriage and sex within marriage as "very good" (Gen 1:27-31; 2:18-25). And then God defined marriage for all cultures and all generations: "For this reason a man will leave his father and mother and be united to his wife, and they will become one flesh" (Genesis 2:24). In Romans 1:18-20, Paul explained that God has revealed some amazing truths about Himself that we can and should all understand through the things that He created, in particular about His "eternal power and divine nature." It is easy to see a lot about God's "eternal power" through

His creation. David wrote about that when he looked at the sun and the stars: "The heavens declare the glory of God; the skies proclaim the work of His hands" (Psalm 19:1). But where do we learn about God's divine nature? God has revealed in the Bible that He is holy and just and good and all powerful and also loving and gracious and patient. But where do we see God's divine nature revealed in creation. I believe that the best place we can see God's "divine nature" revealed in His creation, especially regarding His love, is in the love and marriage of a man and a woman together. Now obviously sin has messed this up terribly and blurred the message so much. But there is still so much of God's heart of love that shines through in this amazing relationship of a man and a woman who fall in love and give themselves to one another for a lifetime of love and faithfulness and oneness together. I have personally concluded that this love and marriage between a man and a woman are the highest and clearest revelation of God's divine nature of love in His physical creation. And that would explain why the heart of Satan's strategy to mess up this revelation is sexual immorality (when people refuse to know God and glorify Him and give Him thanks, they end up in Satan's counterfeit corruption in all forms of sexual immorality and perversions of God's perfect plan – read Romans 1:21-32 and weep for those who have missed out on the glory of God's creation).

So I believe that God has designed love and marriage and the sexual delights and the joy of oneness as some of the clearest revelations of His divine nature, His perfect love, and the perfect oneness that the Father, Jesus, and the Spirit enjoy together from eternity past to eternity future. And They created us in Their image to enjoy that same love and oneness – us with Them and Them with us and then also with one another, especially in marriage. That's what sin destroyed. And that's what Jesus came to restore, so we can love Them again and be one with Them again (read John 14-17 about Jesus' passion for us to abide in Them and

They in us again and about Jesus's ultimate prayer for us that we would all be one with Them again just as They are one together). So Jesus came to live, die, and rise again, so He could save us from the sin that separates us and then restore us again to that love relationship that the Father, Jesus and the Spirit enjoy together and that we were created to enjoy with Them as well – just like a husband and wife were created to enjoy together.

When God tries to explain to us how much He loves us and how much He longs for us to love Him, He often chooses family relationship terms. God is our Father, and we are His children. Jesus is our Husband, and we are His wife. The Holy Spirit is our Teacher, and we are His students. In Revelation 21-22 that is how God tries to describe what eternity will be like for us as believers in the new heaven and the new earth where we will live in our new bodies together with God forever and ever. Sure there will be streets of gold and no more pain and suffering and no more curse and death. But the heart of what eternity will be like is that we are God's Forever Family – with God as our Father and Jesus as our Husband. We will be on a Family Vacation with our Father that never ends and a Honeymoon with our Husband that never ends!! That's Heaven forever!! So I believe that is what God had designed us to enjoy in His original creation. And because sin totally messed that up, Jesus came to die on the cross for our sins and rise again for our righteousness, so now we can be God's Family again. During this lifetime, the Spirit is teaching us how to be the Father's children who learn to call out again, "Abba, Father," and who learn to live again as His heirs (Romans 8:15-17). And during this lifetime, we are learning how to be Jesus' wife again who learns to submit to His love for us and to live together in this "profound mystery" that ultimately Christ and His church are married and are the ultimate expression of God's plan that "for this reason a man will leave his father and mother and be united to his wife, and the two will become one flesh" (Ephesians 5:22-33).

That's why one of the saddest figures of speech used in the Bible is that when we choose to love someone or something more than we love God, we are actually committing spiritual adultery and breaking God's heart!! In the OT, God used this often to describe how He felt when He saw His people bowing down before other gods and worshiping them. In Isaiah 54:5, God said, "For your Maker is your husband – the Lord Almighty is His name." He went on to say that the "Lord will call you back, as if you were a wife deserted and distressed in spirit – a wife who married young, only to be rejected…. For a brief moment I abandoned you, but with deep compassion I will bring you back." In Jeremiah 2-3 God described in regard to Israel how He remembered "the devotion of your youth, how as a bride you loved Me and followed Me through the desert." But then they gave themselves over to prostitution and committed adultery with the many gods and goddesses of the nations around them. Because of their adultery and unfaithfulness, God issued a certificate of divorce first to Israel (the northern ten tribes taken captive by Assyria) and then to her sister Judah (the southern two tribes taken captive by Babylon) and sent them away "because of all her adulteries." Even then God still called out to them, "Return, faithless people, for I am your husband" (3:14). The book of Hosea is all about God seeing Israel as His wife, who left Him and turned back to prostitution. But even after breaking God's heart, God was seeking for her to return and be His wife again. And someday God will welcome Israel back when they turn to Him in repentance and look on Jesus as the One they have pierced and accept Him as their Messiah (Zechariah 12:10 with God's redemption in Zechariah 14). And in the New Testament James called people adulteresses (the best Greek manuscripts just have the feminine word here) whenever they choose to be friends of this world and thus to become enemies of God (James 4:4). I was deeply convicted several years ago when I read 1 John 2:15-17 about the love of the world that keeps us from loving God. Loving this world or being a friend of this world is any way we live according to the "desires of the flesh (sinful nature), the desires of the eyes, and the pride of life." And I realized that Paul talked a lot about Christians living in the flesh, when they are simply living by what makes sense to them, even in their attempts to please God by keeping the law in their own strength (Romans 7:13-8:8; Galatians 5:16-6:8; Philippians 3:1-11). So that really convicted me that I can commit spiritual adultery when I am living for the desires of my flesh, such as by putting my confidence in my efforts to please God and keep His law – even good things like my education or my working long hard hours for God. I can commit spiritual adultery when I look at a bigger church than mine and allow myself to be jealous of them or to decide to be like them so I can be big like they are. I can commit spiritual adultery when I worry about what people think of me and try to do things to impress people because I am more worried about what people think of me as their pastor than what they think about Jesus as their Lord. In the NT, Paul described covetousness or greed (literally "the desire to have more") as idolatry (Ephesians 5:5; Colossians 3:5). It's easy to look at Israel and Judah and condemn them for breaking God's heart with their adultery. But we need to allow the Spirit of God to take us to the mirror of the image of Jesus and be broken with how far short we fall of His glory and to realize how often we too break God's heart with our spiritual adultery.

Now one of the things I have seen people wrestle with is whether the Bible says we are married to Jesus already or whether we don't get married until we get to heaven. One possibility is that our relationship to Jesus as our Husband is so deep and complex that there might be some times where the Bible talks about us like being engaged and other times like us being married. But I personally have concluded that the best way to read the Scripture is that we are already married to Jesus. I believe that Jesus made the great proposal at the cross, as He proved His ultimate love for us once and for all. The Holy Spirit comes to draw us to Jesus and His great love for us. When we accept Jesus as our personal Lord and Savior, we are married to Him as we commit ourselves to one another for an eternity. Here are some of the reasons I lean so strongly in that direction. I believe that Paul defined it that way in Ephesians 5:22-33 when he said that Jesus is already our Husband and Head, and we are already submitting to Him as His wife in everything. Jesus is already in the process of cleansing us of all the filth and ugliness of sin and giving us a total makeover so we become more and more totally beautiful in His sight all the time (this is opposite of how human marriages work where we usually get married at the peak of our physical beauty and strength – and it's all downhill from there). This marriage of Christ and His church is a great mystery, but we can accept it and enjoy it! In Romans 7:4-6, Paul wrote that we died to the law (our old husband) so now we can be married ("become") to a new husband, even Jesus, in order that we may bear fruit to God (possibly all the fruit we bear to God is the result of our union with Jesus as our Husband). In 1 Corinthians 6:12-20 Paul told us to flee from sexual immorality because our bodies are now members of the body of Christ. And if we join our bodies to someone in sexual immorality, we actually become "one with her in body," just as the Bible says, "The two will become one flesh." Then Paul said, "But he who unites himself with the Lord is one with Him in spirit" (6:17). This clarifies that whatever "sexual" union we have with the Lord is totally on a spiritual level, not a physical. But it does say that we have this spiritual sexual union with the Lord. And just like the physical sexual union is at the heart of a man and a woman becoming truly one together, so this spiritual sexual union of us with the Lord is at the heart of us becoming one together with Jesus. This is how God defines marriage: leave parents, join with mate, and become one flesh, where no longer two but now one (Genesis 2:24; Matthew 19:4-6; Ephesians 5:32). And since I personally believe the Bible says that God's plan for enjoying sexual union is only within the relationship of marriage as a husband and a wife, I believe that God would be talking about us as believers enjoying a spiritual sexual union with the Lord only within a marriage bond that has already occurred. In 2 Corinthians 11:2-3, Paul said that he had already joined them in marriage to one husband that he may present them as a pure virgin to Christ. The Greek word used here is translated "to fit, fit in; to fit together, join, harmonize; to join or give in marriage." Some translations have been unfortunate in that they picked up on the culture of that time that often tied the giving in marriage even back to the time of the legal contract of "betrothal" or promising in marriage (what we could call engagement today). And if this were the only passage on the subject, that could be a possible understanding. But since the heart of the word is "to fit together, join, give in marriage," I believe it is best to translate it that way in this passage as well. Paul's desire to "present them as a pure virgin" is talking about how we are living as Christians today in a "sincere and pure devotion to Christ," instead of being deceived by Satan to commit spiritual adultery where we are loving and choosing what we want for our selfish pleasure rather than what Jesus wants for our pleasure together.

So when we turn to Revelation 19:7-9, here is what I believe Jesus was telling John. I believe that we are married to Christ the moment we accept Him as our personal Lord and Savior. He came into our world and died on a cross for our sins to win us back to Himself and His love for us. When we accept His love and share our marriage vows together, we become Husband and wife. And we begin to enjoy our spiritual sexual union and spiritual oneness together. Unfortunately, we still carry a lot of baggage from our old life. And at times we may still commit spiritual adultery and break His heart. And many times we refuse to submit to His headship and love in our lives. But our spiritual lives down here on planet earth are all about learning to become "pure virgins" whose hearts are totally, passionately in love with Christ and Christ alone. And He is constantly working in our hearts toward that goal of cleansing us of all the unrighteousness and ugliness of sin and making us truly holy and righteous just like He is. But we are still in a war zone, and Satan as our enemy does not give up easily. So we are constantly making those choices to turn from Satan and to choose to love and follow Jesus as our Husband in everything. When this life is over and we enter into God's presence, that is when we can finally have the big wedding celebration in heaven with all the believers of the ages as the Bride of Christ. At some point of time there will be the judgment seat of Christ when all the wood, hay and straw of what we did in our sinful flesh and in our self-righteousness will be burned up and destroyed in the fire and what all that we allowed Jesus to do in and through us to make us truly holy and righteous will be purified and rewarded with eternal rewards (1 Corinthians 3:12-15). That may well be the time where we as His wife (word used here is "wife, woman") have made ourselves ready (Revelation 19:7-9). That is when we are given the "fine linen, bright and clean … fine linen stands for the righteous acts of the saints." This righteousness is completely the righteousness of Christ not our self-righteousness of the law (Philippians 3:6, 9). The focus of what takes place here is the "wedding supper of the Lamb," that great feast where the Father throws the ultimate wedding reception in honor of His Son and the great rescue and salvation of His wife!! This might even take place on earth following Christ's return to the earth when He establishes His kingdom on the earth for 1,000 years (guests might be those who enter that kingdom as believers). Then our eternal honeymoon in the New Heaven and New Earth doesn't begin until those 1,000 years are over, and sin, Satan, death, and hell are thrown into the Lake of Fire for eternal destruction (Revelation 20-22). So I see three phases of our marriage to Christ: we are married at the moment of salvation and begin our relationship as Husband and wife, we attend the great Wedding Supper of the Lamb where the Father throws the ultimate feast in celebration of the Greatest Love Story of the Universe, and then later we go on our Eternal Honeymoon in the New Heaven and New Earth.

With this freedom of seeing myself already married to Jesus, I can delight in the imagery of a passionate, intimate love relationship with Jesus. I can see Him as my Husband loving me with all His heart and soul and mind and strength and Him helping me as His wife to love Him in return in that same way. I can see Him as my Husband longing to be joined with me in a spiritual sexual union that fills us both with ultimate passion and pleasure. Just as human sexual desire and pleasure may be life's highest delight, so spiritual sexual desire and pleasure may be the highest delight for us and our Lord, where we are both filled with a joy inexpressible and full of glory (1 Peter 1:8). And I can see Him as my Husband longing to be truly ONE with me and me with Him as the ultimate fulfillment and enjoyment of true love where we are totally bound together in perfect oneness in every level of life (this is what Jesus prayed for the night before going to the cross – that we would be one with Him just as He and the Father enjoy one another in perfect oneness and perfect love – John 17:20-26).

Over the years I have discovered the delightful reality from what Paul talked about in Ephesians 5:22-33 that the more I study Jesus and how He loves me as His wife, the more it helps me to understand how to love my wife. And the more I study how I love and delight myself in my wife, the more I understand how much Jesus loves me and delights Himself in me. And the more I think of how and why we as believers long to submit to Jesus in everything, the more it helps me to know how to lead my wife to that point where she wants to submit to me in everything as well. And the more I think of what all my wife does to love and please and delight me, the more I understand what all I can do to love and please and delight my Lord. And the more I think about how much my wife and I long to be joined together sexually and even more how much we long to be totally ONE together in every dimension of our lives, the more I understand how much Jesus and we as believers long to be joined together in a passionate ecstasy of spiritual sexual union and how much even more we long to become truly ONE together where we live and work together in perfect Oneness in every dimension of our lives.

No wonder Satan tries so hard to twist and distort human love, oneness and sexuality because the true love, oneness and sexual pleasure of a husband and wife may be God's clearest picture in all of His physical creation of the love and oneness and spiritual sexual pleasure that He longs to have with us and we long to have with Him.

Of course, there is an even greater revelation of how much God loves us: God demonstrated His love for us when Jesus went to the cross to die for our sins. This is an even more powerful demonstration of the greatest love of all. It's that love that moves us to believe that God loves us with such a perfect love that we can trust and accept that love!! And when we do, that is when we find out that it is truly God's love that we have wanted all along more than anything else – to know we love and are loved by the God of eternity now and forever!!

FINDING REAL SUCCESS
Chapter 11

As a kid I loved backyard sports, especially when I scored the points and my team won. That's how I knew I was a success. And I loved even more excelling in academics, especially when I got the good grades and the high rankings. That's how I knew I was a success. But when I became a pastor, I wasn't sure how to know when I was a success. Society says it is defined by growing congregations, bigger budgets and buildings, national recognition, increased impact. But I haven't found those things in Scripture. And even what I experienced of them didn't satisfy.

Instead I have become intrigued with the realization that God says true spiritual success is identified by how much we are becoming like Jesus in holiness and righteousness in the truth. I have been amazed how many times it talks in both the Old and New Testaments about how righteousness is what God wants to see in our lives. For example, in the Sermon on the Mount Jesus said, "Blessed are those who hunger and thirst for righteousness, for they shall be filled" (Matthew 5:6) and "But seek first [present command – indicating continuous action] God's kingdom and righteousness, and all these things will be added to you" (Matthew 6:33). At the end of his ministry, Paul wrote that we should pursue, strive for, seek after, run after righteousness, godliness, faith ... (1 Timothy 6:11; 2 Timothy 2:22).

Righteousness is simply thinking, doing, saying what is right according to God's standards. God wants us simply to pursue righteousness as the passion of our lives. That is why it is so important to know how to discern the difference between right and wrong and how to choose and live the right.

Where righteousness comes from. We can see in Romans 1:16-17 that the focus of the whole book of Romans is that the righteousness of God is revealed in the gospel from faith unto faith, because the righteous one shall live by faith. This is compared to the wrath of God being revealed against the ungodliness and unrighteousness of men. For the rest of the book Paul wrote about how God declares us righteous at our salvation (justification) and then how He makes us righteous throughout the rest of our lives (sanctification) and then how He makes us fully righteous in heaven (glorification). In 4:25 Paul explained that Jesus died for ours sins and was raised for our righteousness or justification. The power is all of Jesus to deliver us from our sins and to produce in us His righteousness. In 6:1-23 Paul wrote that now we have died unto sin and are alive unto God where we can live in righteousness. Now that we live under grace and no longer under law, we are no longer slaves to sin leading to death but we are slaves unto righteousness leading to life to the full now and forever. Just as the wages of sin is death, so the gift of God is eternal life in Christ Jesus our Lord. And in 7:1-8:8 Paul said that we no longer live under works of law in the power of flesh, leading to the frustration of constant failure and defeat by living under law. Instead we now live by faith in God's grace in the power of the Holy Spirit, leading to the freedom to live where the righteous requirements of the law are fully met in us (8:4). The ultimate good toward which God is working all things in our lives (even the bad things) is that we become more and more conformed to the image of His Son Jesus all the time (8:28-29).

In Ephesians Paul wrote over and over again about holiness as well as righteousness. God chose us in Christ to be holy and blameless before Him in love as His adopted sons (1:4). Jesus is teaching us that we should no longer walk like the pagans do, but instead we should walk as those who have been created to be like God in righteousness and holiness of the truth (4:17-24). We walk in the light now, and the fruit or evidence of walking in the light is in all goodness and righteousness and truth (5:8-14). Jesus not only laid down His life to save us, but now He lives to make us holy, cleansing us and making us beautiful, so that we will be holy and blameless (5:25-27). This impacts every area of our lives and relationships as we put off the old ways of living and put on the new ways of righteousness and holiness and truth (see all of Ephesians 4-6).

In Philippians we see that this righteousness God is talking about is always the righteousness of God that Christ produces in us as we come to Him by faith and not our self-righteousness by the law (Philippians 3:3-11). Paul was clear that his self-righteousness was like so much manure or rubbish compared to the glory of the righteousness of God that Jesus was producing in him. Under the new covenant of grace, God has provided the power through His Son Jesus, so that now Jesus can produce in us the very righteousness and holiness of God Himself.

Over the years God kept using His Word to lead me to this conclusion that the real standard of success in God's eyes is how much we become holy and righteous in the truth through the power of Christ living in us. This true spiritual success is what can give us the assurance in this lifetime that we truly are God's child and that Jesus truly is living and working in us to bring every area of our lives into submission under Him (1 John 3:4-10). And this is what gives us hope as we face the future judgment that we will have eternal rewards for all the righteousness that we allow Jesus to produce in us. Jesus showed to John as he wrote the book of Revelation that the wedding garments for us as believers who are the bride of Christ will be the righteous acts that we have done in this lifetime (Revelation 19:8). I personally believe that what passes through the fire of the judgment seat of Christ as true gold, silver and precious stones that will bring us eternal rewards is the righteousness we let Christ produce in us (1 Corinthians 3:11-15 – compared to the filthy rags of our righteousness that will be burned in the fire). And these are probably the crowns we will cast at His feet to show off His glory forever (Revelation 4:10-11)!!

That is why God calls us to get passionate about righteousness, to hunger and thirst after righteousness, to seek first the kingdom of God and His righteousness, to pursue righteousness. That's how we know we are a true success in God's eyes when we become more and more like Christ in His holiness and righteousness in His truth. And what a relief it is to know that Christ living in us is the One who leads us to His righteousness, holiness, and truth through the power of His death, resurrection, and exaltation.

What a difference righteousness makes. Trying to find righteousness through the law keeps us focused on our sin. The law tells us all the things we can't do and all the things we have to do. And it keeps showing us how much we sin and fail to meet up to these standards. And that keeps us under condemnation and guilt and fear before a holy God. So we have to keep offering all kinds of sacrifices for our sins to be able to find God's forgiveness. And then we have to do that all over again the next time we sin. That keeps us obsessed with writing all kinds of rules and building all kinds of fences to keep us from crossing the line into sin. And that keeps us debating where those lines are and how close we can get to the lines before we fall into sin. That is what Pharisees did with the Law of Moses and what so many people still do today.

But trying to find righteousness through grace keeps us excited with Jesus and how He is making us holy and righteous just like He is. Grace tells us we are completely and forever forgiven of our sins through the blood of Jesus. And now we are being freed from the power and bondage of those sins to the degree that we let Christ break those bondages in our lives. And ultimately grace even enables us to forget our sins – because God has!!! We are no longer slaves to sin. We have died to sin, and we have been freed from sin. We don't have to live under sin any longer. Now grace sets us free to focus on the power of Christ to conform us to His image, to make us holy and righteous with the very holiness and righteousness of God, to help us walk in the light of God's truth just like Jesus does.

And now whatever battles and bondages we face, we believe that Jesus can free us. We have the confidence of victory as we see the power of Christ living in us. Just as Jesus has helped us in the past, He will help us in the future. And we believe that no matter what comes, we can do all things through Christ who gives us strength (Philippians 4:13). We are more than conquerors through Christ who loves us (Romans 8:37). We are always marching in triumphal procession with Jesus (2 Corinthians 2:14).

So now rather than focusing on sin and debating how close we can get to the lines without crossing them, we focus on righteousness and how close we can get to the holiness and righteousness of Christ in truth. We have heard about how people are trained to identify counterfeit money. They study the real thing so intensely that whenever they see a counterfeit they know it right away. The more we pursue righteousness and live it, the more we instantly recognize the counterfeit of sin and flee from it.

Think of Adam and Eve in the Garden. Satan led them to focus on the one tree they couldn't have instead of the thousands of trees they could have. That's still how Satan works today. Think of how that brought death to them and to everyone else who has ever lived since then. But in contrast think of Jesus and how He lived His entire life – He lived for the passion of doing whatever His Father wanted Him to do from the beginning to the end, even to the point of death. Think of how that has brought life back to our world for all who believe in Jesus as their Lord and Savior.

For example, rather than debating about sexual immorality and how much we can get away with or how far we can go, we just get passionate about enjoying our sexuality the way God created us to enjoy it in holiness and righteousness and truth. We focus so much on thinking and doing what is right that the thought of doing what is wrong is unthinkable to us.

The good news of the gospel is that because of the death of Christ in our place, we have died to sin, we have been set free from sin, and sin is no longer our master. And now because of the resurrection of Christ, we have been raised to a new life where we can live unto righteousness, where we can be slaves to righteousness, where we just naturally do what is right through the power of Christ living in us. And this is the good news for everyone around us – they can get it right too!!!

Our job is not to tell people in the darkness how dark their world is and to condemn them for walking in that dark world. Instead our job is to point them to Jesus as the Light of the world who can deliver them too from Satan's kingdom of darkness and death and bring them into God's kingdom of light and life forever. That is the exciting truth of John 3:16-17. God did not send Jesus into our world to condemn the world but to save the world through Him. And we are sent into our world in the same way! Unfortunately Christians and churches too often condemn and judge people, as they look down on sinners and make them feel guilty. Instead we desperately need to learn to live in righteousness and holiness and truth. That is how we turn on the light and let others see and understand how much better righteousness is than sin, how much better life is than death. Then we can tell them how they can come to Jesus to find the same salvation, light, freedom, and life we are enjoying. We can tell them how they can be saved from the horror of Satan's kingdom of the darkness and death that sin brings and be welcomed into God's kingdom of the light and life that righteousness brings!!

That is why God calls us to get passionate about righteousness, to hunger and thirst after righteousness, to seek first the kingdom of

God and His righteousness, to pursue righteousness all through the power of Christ living in us because that is when we will find the true victory and freedom that only Jesus can produce in us. We will no longer be saying what Paul said when he tried to find righteousness through the law, "What a wretched man I am! Who will rescue me from this body of death?" (Rom 7:24). Instead we will be saying, "Thanks be to God – through Jesus Christ our Lord!" (Rom 7:25). And what a difference that makes!! And we can invite others to join us in that same freedom!!

We can become like Jesus!! This is really the ultimate goal, becoming righteous and holy in God's truth – just like Jesus is. God has predestined us to "be conformed to the likeness of His Son," and that is the ultimate good toward which God is working everything in our lives (Romans 8:28-29). The real glory of the new covenant is that now we can behold as in a mirror the glory of the Lord and be transformed into His image from glory unto glory by the power of the Spirit of the Lord (2 Corinthians 3:18). That is not the passing glory of the law that is fading away. But this is the eternal glory of grace that never passes away. And now we are no longer blinded by Satan or veiled by law. Now we can see with unveiled face the "light of the gospel of the glory of Christ" (2 Corinthians 4:4). Now God has made His light shine in our hearts to give us the light of the knowledge of the glory of God in the face of Christ (2 Corinthians 4:6). When Moses was on Mount Sinai seeing the glory of God, he was only allowed to see the back of God in all His glory, not the face (Exodus 33:18-23). But now under grace, we can actually see the fullness of the glory of God in the face of Christ. And it is our privilege to be transformed into this image of God from glory unto glory in all righteousness and holiness in truth!!

It is intriguing to think that if sin is any way we fall short of the glory of God (Romans 3:23), the righteousness of God that Jesus produces in us is how we are restored to the glory of God. This is what we as new creations in Christ can expect – that Jesus is constantly working in us to help us become more and more like God in righteousness and holiness in truth (Ephesians 4:24). That is why Paul wrote that our ultimate goal as a church is for all of us to be ministering together in such a way that we are "attaining to the whole measure of the fullness of Christ" (Ephesians 4:11-13).

So really the choice is very simple: 1) sin can be our master leading to death, and the more we focus on sin the more we will experience the pain and suffering of spiritual disease and death or 2) righteousness can be our master leading to life, and the more we focus on the righteousness that only Christ can produce in us the more we will find the freedom of spiritual health and stamina and life to the full now and forever. God invites us to pursue righteousness and find life. God invites us to the thrilling adventure of finding life by seeking first the kingdom of God and His righteousness, by hungering and thirsting after righteousness, by living our lives to pursue and seek to find and live the very righteousness of God by faith in Jesus.

This is real success – becoming like Jesus in all of His righteousness and holiness in His truth through the power of Christ living in us and then letting that light shine so brilliantly that we will stimulate others to want to join us in that success as well!!

SHOWING OFF JESUS
Chapter 12

I remember a very special time when I was meditating on the book of Philippians (especially 2:6-13) that the Spirit excited me with the realization that possibly the greatest way we can bring pleasure to God is when we join Him in His sheer delight of exalting His Son Jesus. That must have been the Father's greatest pain as He watched His Son become obedient to His Father's will to death, even death on a cross. Even though that had been Their plan since before They created mankind, that was the ultimate sacrifice of ultimate love for the Father to place all our sins upon His Son and to allow His Son to pay the penalty of our sins by dying in our place for our salvation. But then that must have been the most exciting moment of all eternity for the Father when He raised His Son from the dead in the greatest victory in the entire universe for all eternity. From the greatest agony to the greatest ecstasy all in three days!! THEREFORE, God has exalted His Son Jesus to the highest place and given Him the Name that is above every name. And now God's greatest desire for us may well be that at the name of Jesus we should bow the knee in humble submission and confess with our tongue and live with our lives the reality that truly Jesus Christ is Lord!! That may be how we bring God His greatest glory. And what excited me that day as I was meditating on this passage is that I saw the connection of the next verses with what Paul had just written. God is working in us to will and to do what brings Him His good pleasure, and we are simply to be working out this amazing salvation that He is working in us with fear and trembling. And I realized that possibly what brings God his greatest pleasure is when we join Him in exalting His Son Jesus as we submit to His control as Lord of every part of our lives by allowing Him to unleash in us all the power of His death, His resurrection and His exaltation however He wants.

It is exciting that we get to live for God's glory as the new creation in Christ Jesus. The first creation showed off the glory of God in His physical creation ("The heavens declare the glory of God," Psalm 19:1). But now God's new creation shows off the glory of God in His spiritual creation. And we are that new creation ("If anyone is in Christ, he is a new creation," 2 Corinthians 5:17). So we show off God's glory every way that we let Jesus save us from Satan enslaving us under sin, death and hell and every way that we let Jesus as Lord give us His righteousness, life and heaven. So whenever we allow Jesus to unleash in us the power of His death (freeing us from sin and death), the power of His resurrection (freeing us for righteousness and life), and the power of His exaltation (leading us to victory over Satan and his control in our lives), that is how we exalt Jesus and show off the glory of God in our lives.

In the Book of Ephesians, Paul points us to this great privilege we have of living for the glory of God by receiving the riches of God's grace unleashed in us through the work of Jesus in our lives. God the Father has chosen us as His family and blessed us and made us holy and redeemed us and poured out all the riches of His grace upon us and given us His Spirit so that we can be "to the praise of the glory of His grace" (1:6, 12, 14). Because of His great love for us, God has made us alive with Christ when He saved us by His grace, and now He has raised us with Christ and exalted us with Christ in the heavenlies in order that for the ages of eternity God may be able to show the incomparable riches of His grace, expressed in His kindness to us in Christ Jesus. That is the ultimate goal of God saving us by His grace, of God making us His masterpiece, of God creating us in Christ Jesus to do those good works God prepared in advance for us to do is so that now and forever we can show off the incomparable riches of His grace, expressed to us in His kindness to us in Christ Jesus (2:4-10). In fact, the good works that God has prepared in advance for us to do may simply be ways we live to show off the glory of God's grace unleashed in our lives, as we allow Jesus as Lord to work in us in all the power of His death, His resurrection, and His exaltation. God's eternal purpose that He has accomplished in Christ Jesus our Lord is that now through us as the church the multifaceted wisdom of God should be made known to the supernatural beings of the heavenlies (both good and evil – 3:10-11). God is able to do and wants to do immeasurably more than all we can ask or imagine, through this power of Christ living in us, so that God may be glorified in the church and in Christ Jesus throughout all generations for all the ages of eternity (3:20-21).

No wonder Satan tries so hard to get us living in our works trying to please God and keep His law by our efforts of flesh, because then we are living for our glory so that we can have a reason to boast (Ephesians 2:8-9; Romans 4:1-4). We are such proud, selfish people that we are so easily tempted to want to do our works and achieve our righteousness by our own flesh efforts, so that we can get at least some of the glory. We want to be able to boast about ourselves and what we have done and are doing for God. But that is why the Bible is so clear that we are all sinners who cannot save ourselves. And any attempts we have to achieve righteousness by the law are really filthy rags or so much rubbish or manure (Isaiah 64:6; Philippians 3:8). God calls us to be saved by faith in His grace through the power of His Spirit and to live that same way and to minister that same way as we become holy and righteous in the truth through the power of Jesus alive and living in us – so that all the glory goes to God and God alone. That is why the worship of heaven always acknowledges that God alone deserves all the glory and honor and power and praise because the Father and the Son and the Spirit have DONE ALL THE WORK (Revelation 4:11; 5:9-14).

I have concluded that probably the biggest battle they faced in the early church and that Paul and the other apostles had to keep addressing was this temptation to live under works of law in the energy of the flesh so that they could still have some reason to boast and to get at least some of the glory. That is why the New Testament is filled with teachings about how we must no longer live under works of law in the energy of the flesh but that we must live by faith in Jesus and His grace through the power of the Holy Spirit now living in us. And this is not just for that point of time when we receive Jesus as our Lord and Savior but for every moment of our lives on planet earth and for all of eternity. And I suspect this is still the heart of the biggest battle we face as believers today. Satan knows that all he has to do to keep us from experiencing the power of Christ living and working in and through us is to get us back living under law. Then Christ will be of no value to us at all, we will be obligated to obey the whole law, we have been alienated from Christ, and we have fallen from grace (Galatians 5:2-4). That is why it is so imperative that we walk in the freedom that Christ has brought us, the freedom of living by faith in Jesus in God's grace provided by Jesus through the power of the Holy Spirit (Galatians 5:1).

Now this gives us a radically different perspective on all the power and bondage of sin in our lives and also on all the suffering and disappointment in our lives, as these actually give us opportunities to bring more praise to the glory of God's grace. It is interesting that there are two major places where the Bible says God's grace can shine brightly for God's glory – in our sins and in our sufferings. In Romans 5:20-21, Paul wrote that "where sin increased grace increased all the more, so that just as sin reigned in death, so also grace might reign through righteousness to bring eternal life through Jesus Christ our Lord." There is no sin that God's grace is not greater still. Now we never sin that grace may abound. God forbid!!! (Romans 6:1-2) But no matter how much we have sinned and how deep that bondage to sin may be in our lives, these areas just give us a chance to see how much greater grace really is. This is where we can show off that much more the power of Jesus unleashing His grace in our lives not only delivering us from that sin but also leading us to the very righteousness and holiness of Jesus. Then in 2 Corinthians 12:7-10 Paul talked about his thorn in the flesh and how he begged God to remove it. But God didn't. Instead God said to Paul, "My grace is sufficient for you, for My power is made perfect in weakness." Paul responded, "Therefore I will boast all the more gladly about my weaknesses, so that Christ's power may rest on me." Paul applied that not only to his suffering with that thorn but also to all the opposition and persecution he was experiencing. So the sharper the thorns and the greater the suffering and persecution in our lives, the greater the opportunity we have to experience God's grace and to show off Jesus unleashing His grace in our lives and perfecting His power in our weakness!!

I have personally concluded that this is the test that determines our eternal rewards. Those things that we have done in works of law in energy of flesh for our glory are the wood, hay, and straw that will be burned in the fire at the judgment seat of Christ. But those things that we have done by faith in Jesus as we live under grace through the power of the Spirit for God's glory, those are the pure gold, silver, and precious stones that will pass the test of fire and bring us eternal rewards (1 Corinthians 3:12-15). And even though these may be the crowns we cast at the feet of Jesus (Revelation 4:10), they are still rewards that will impact our lives for an eternity (Matthew 5:10-12; 25:21, 23, 26-30).

So God the Father invites us to join Him in what may well be His highest pleasure – exalting His Son Jesus and leading us and others to celebrate His name as above every name as we bow the knee in total submission to confess with our mouths and live with our lives the reality that truly Jesus Christ is Lord!! This probably is what brings God His greatest glory and His greatest pleasure!! That means we bring Him our sins, our bondages, our weaknesses, those spiritual strongholds Satan has built in our lives; and we let Jesus save us and set us free to live in righteousness, holiness, and truth by the power of His grace. That means we bring Him our suffering, our disappointments, our weaknesses as well as those doubts and struggles we face because of the persecution and rejection and opposition of those around us, and we let Jesus perfect His power in our weakness by the power of His grace. And we do all this realizing that this is how we show off the glory of God and His grace in our world today and in the world to come for all of eternity. What a thrilling privilege to live our lives to the praise of the glory of God and His grace by exalting Jesus as Lord of all, as we simply come to Jesus by faith to allow Him to live and work in us in all the power of His death, His resurrection, and His exaltation!!

TAUGHT BY GOD
Chapter 13

One of the most exciting truths that has radically changed my life and ministry is that God Himself is teaching me. It was what Jesus said in John 10 that really opened my eyes to this truth. Jesus explained that He is the Good Shepherd, and we as believers are His sheep. Obviously the most thrilling thing Jesus said is that He came to lay down His life for us as His sheep, so He could rescue us from the one who comes only to steal, kill and destroy and so that instead He could give us life, life to the full (verse 10). But the truth that I missed so long is that Jesus as our Shepherd speaks to us, and we as His sheep hear His voice and follow Him. In fact, He calls us by name, so that means He speaks to us personally, individually, uniquely and says to us just exactly what we need to hear. And we can tell the difference between His voice and Satan's voice. Jesus was talking not just about His twelve disciples but also about all of us as the "other sheep" who will also hear His voice. So this passage has excited me so much with the truth that all of us as believers are able to hear Jesus speaking to us and then to follow Him as He leads us into the fullness of the life that He came to give us.

Since then I have seen many other passages that confirm that our God is speaking to us and teaching us constantly. And we are able to hear His voice and learn from Him and follow Him as He leads us into all truth. It is interesting that some passages talk about the Father teaching us, some about Jesus teaching us, and some about the Holy Spirit teaching us. This is such amazing grace that the God of heaven actually cares enough about each one of us as individuals that the Father, Son, and Holy Spirit are all speaking into our lives.

Here are some Scriptures that reinforce this truth that we as believers are taught by God Himself.

- Jesus said, "I praise You, Father ... because you have hidden these things from the wise and learned, and revealed them to little children. Yes, Father, for this was your good pleasure. All things have been committed to Me by My Father. No one knows the Son except the Father, and no one knows the Father except the Son and those to whom the Son chooses to reveal Him" (Matthew 11:25-27).
- Jesus said, "No one can come to Me unless the Father who sent Me draws him.... It is written in the Prophets: 'They will all be taught by God.' Everyone who listens to the Father and learns from Him comes to Me" (John 6:44-45).
- Jesus said, "The sheep listen to His voice. He calls His own sheep by name and leads them out ... His sheep follow Him because they know His voice ... I know My sheep and My sheep know Me ... the other sheep will listen to My voice ... My sheep listen to My voice; I know them, and they follow Me" (John 10:3-4, 14, 16, 27).
- Jesus said, "But I, when I am lifted up from the earth, will draw all men to Myself" (John 12:32).
- Jesus said, "He who loves Me will be loved by My Father, and I too will love him and show Myself to him.... My Father will love him, and we will come to him and make our home with him" (John 14:21, 23).
- Jesus said about the Holy Spirit, "He will teach you all things and will remind you of everything I have said to you.... The Spirit of truth will testify about Me.... It is for your good that I am going away. Unless I go away, the Counselor will not come to you, but if I go, I will send Him to you. When He comes, He will convict the world of guilt in regard to sin and righteousness and judgment.... When He, the Spirit of truth, comes, He will guide you into all truth. He will not speak on

His own, He will speak only what He hears, and He will tell you what is yet to come. He will bring glory to Me by taking from what is Mine and making it known to you. All that belongs to the Father is Mine. That is why I said the Spirit will take from what is Mine and make it known to you." (John 14:26; 15:26; 16:7-15). [Here is an intriguing thought from John 16:12-15: three times Jesus used the same word "to reveal ("tell" or "make it known" in NIV)." The Spirit will reveal the coming things (verse 13), He will take the things that are Jesus' and reveal them to us (verse 14), and He takes the things that are Jesus' and that are also the Father's and reveal them to us (verse 15). I would suggest that the "coming things" of verse 13 are simply the things that Jesus and the Father have and that They give to the Spirit each day to give to us – to guide us into all truth!!! That is a thrilling prospect!! The Spirit is revealing to us what Jesus has for us for today – not what Jesus will have for us some day in the distant future.]

- "Be transformed by the renewing of your mind. Then you will be able to test and approve what God's will is – His good, pleasing and perfect will" (Romans 12:2).
- "'No eye has seen, no ear has heard, no mind has conceived what God has prepared for those who love Him' – but God has revealed it to us by His Spirit.... No one knows the thoughts of God except the Spirit of God. We have not received the spirit of this world but the Spirit who is from God, that we may understand what God has freely given us. This is what we speak, not in words taught us by human wisdom but in words taught by the Spirit, expressing spiritual truths in spiritual words.... But we have the mind of Christ" (1 Corinthians 2:9-13, 16). [Another intriguing thought is that the things "no eye has seen ..." are not talking about heaven someday but about what Jesus has provided for us in the New Covenant – because "God has revealed it to us by His Spirit." This is present reality not future hope.]

- "And we, who with unveiled faces all behold as in a mirror [NIV, "reflect"] the Lord's glory, are being transformed into His likeness, with ever-increasing glory, which comes from the Lord, who is the Spirit.... For God, who said, 'Let light shine out of darkness,' made His light shine in our hearts to give us the light of the knowledge of the glory of God in the face of Christ" (2 Corinthians 3:18; 4:6).
- "For we are God's workmanship, created in Christ Jesus to do good works, which God prepared in advance for us to do" (Ephesians 2:10).
- "You were taught ... to be made new in the attitude of your minds, and to put on the new self, created to be like God in righteousness and holiness of the truth" (Ephesians 4:20-24).
- "It is God who works in you to will and to act according to His good purpose" (Philippians 2:13).
- "And have put on the new self, which is being renewed in knowledge in the image of its Creator" (Colossians 3:10).
- God said about the New Covenant of grace: "I will put my laws in their minds and write them on their hearts. I will be their God, and they will be My people. No longer will a man teach his neighbor, or a man his brother, saying, 'Know the Lord,' because they will all know Me, from the least of them to the greatest" (Hebrews 8:10-11).
- "May the God of peace ... equip you with everything good for doing His will, and may He work in us what is pleasing to Him through Jesus Christ, to Whom be glory for ever and ever. Amen" (Hebrews 12:20-21).
- "But you have an Anointing from the Holy One, and all of you know the truth.... As for you, the Anointing you received from Him remains in you, and you do not need anyone to teach you. But as His Anointing teaches you about all things, and as that Anointing is real, not counterfeit – just as it has taught you, remain in Him" (1 John 2:20, 27).

This is amazing – God is still speaking to us today. God is our Father, and we are His children. Jesus is our Husband, and we are His wife. The Spirit is our Teacher, and we are His students. It should be obvious that God is constantly speaking to us – the Father, Jesus, and the Spirit. What father doesn't speak to his children? What husband doesn't speak to his wife? What teacher doesn't speak to his students? That's what they do. That's who they are. Even so with God!! What isn't as obvious to us is that we can hear Them speaking, and we can obey Their voice and follow Them wherever They lead. They are speaking to all believers, young and old, male and female, educated and uneducated, sophisticated and unsophisticated, liberal and conservative, compliant and rebellious, morally upright and morally depraved. When we accept Jesus Christ as our Lord and Savior, then the Father, Jesus, and the Spirit all begin Their work of radically transforming us in our minds, our attitudes, our desires, our actions, our words, our relationships, our emotions, and everything else that makes up our lives. They are constantly talking to us. And we can hear Them speaking, and we can obey and follow Them.

The Bible is very clear that the way we love God is simply by obeying God as our Father, Jesus as our Lord and Husband, and the Spirit as our Teacher in whatever They say to us (Matthew 28:18-20; John 14:15, 21-24, 31; 15:9-10, 14; Romans 12:1-2; Ephesians 1:9-11, 20-23; 5:22-24; Philippians 2:9-11; 1 John 2:3-6; 5:1-5). Sin is disobedience against God in whatever He says to us. Righteousness is obedience to God in whatever He says to us. Jesus died to deliver us from our sins, so that now He can make us righteous again where we want to hear God speak to us and to obey Him in whatever He says.

I believe that our greatest ministry to one another as believers is to encourage each other to hear God's voice and to obey Him in whatever He says. I find it interesting in some of Jesus' final words before He returned to heaven that He told us our job is to "make disciples [leading people to become followers of Jesus], baptizing them [teaching them to take this early step of obedience], and then teaching them to obey [or 'keep' – same word used in John 14:15, 21, 23-24] all of Jesus' commands" (Matt 28:18-20). Jesus did not command us to teach them all of His commandments, but to teach them to OBEY all His commands. Our primary job is to teach people to OBEY – not to know. A possible thought is that God's job is to teach them to KNOW, our job is to teach them to OBEY. Tragically too often we try to do God's job and ask God to do ours. Maybe that's why so many families and churches are so messed up because so few are truly hearing and obeying Jesus as Lord. So often we teach the Bible stories and repeat Jesus's commands, but we aren't obeying them, even though we may try to tell others they must. What we desperately need is to see people who are passionately obeying Jesus and teaching others to obey Him too.

Now I believe that God does use us as humans to teach His Word, but we are just tools in His hands as He does His job. And we have to give Him the freedom to teach each one of His disciples even if He may lead them to conclusions different than He has led us to. Paul taught in Romans 14:1-15:7 that we may reach different conclusions, but what matters is that we bow before Jesus as Lord and do what we believe He is leading us to do – because some day we will all bow before Jesus as Lord and give Him answer for our obedience or disobedience. The Lord has convicted me so much that I must not let human teachers and leaders pressure me to conform to their man-made rules and regulations, teachings and traditions. Jesus even said that we worship in vain if we do that (Matthew 15:1-9). We must not be living under human teachers with all their rules and regulations because we have died with Christ to those things and have been raised with Christ to a whole new existence where we live with Christ in the heavenlies (Colossians 2:8-3:4). Now we set our hearts and our minds on these things above where the Father, Jesus and the Spirit live and where They are actually the Ones teaching us and leading us to understand and live as citizens now of heaven and not just of earth (Philippians 3:20-21).

So God still speaks today. And those of us who are His children can hear His voice and follow Him. We are called to be people who are taught by God!!! God speaks to us through human teachers that He gives to His church (Ephesians 4:11-16). God speaks to us through this Book He wrote and gave to us (2 Timothy 3:5-17). God speaks to us through the experiences and suffering of life (Romans 8:28-29; 1 Peter 4:1-6). God speaks to us through His Spirit (John 14-17). God still speaks!! And God calls us to dare to believe that He Himself is calling us by name and speaking us. We believers are all being TAUGHT BY GOD, and it is our joy and privilege to hear His voice and follow Him in absolute obedience!!!

FINDING REAL LIFE
Chapter 14

When Jesus prayed to His Father the night before He went to the cross, He obviously was focusing on the heart of what He was doing and why He was going to the cross. He said it was "that He might give eternal life to all those You have given Him" (John 17:2). The ultimate purpose of Christ coming to die and rise again was so He could deliver us from death and give us eternal life now and forever!! Jesus had said over and over again throughout His ministry that He had come into our world to save us from death so He could give us life, life to the full now in this lifetime and forever in the life to come (John 3:16; 5:24; 6:32-58; 10:10; 14:6).

But the big question is "what is life?" Jesus answered that question when He prayed that final night before the cross, "Now this is eternal life: that they may know You, the only true God, and Jesus Christ, Whom You have sent" (John 17:3). And at the end of this prayer Jesus concluded by saying, "Though the world does not know You, I know You, and they [Jesus' disciples] know that You have sent Me. I have made You known to them, and will continue to make You known in order that the love You have for Me may be in Them and that I Myself may be in Them" (John 17:25-26). On that last night before the cross, Jesus had been talking about how to experience the fullness of God's love where we abide in the Father and Jesus and They abide in us (John 14:10-12, 20-23; 15:1-8). This love and intimacy and oneness are what Jesus was praying about when He asked the Father to make us one with Them just as They are one with one another (John 17:20-23). This is the ultimate oneness of knowing and loving God the way God created us and now redeemed us to do (John 17:20-26). I would suggest that Jesus was not praying about us becoming one with one another as believers but about us becoming one with the Father and Jesus just as They are one together. That is when the unbelievers around us will believe that Jesus truly is God's Son sent into our world to save sinners. Of course, those who are truly one with the Father and Jesus will be one with one another as well. Maybe we should just accept that Satan will constantly create disunity in the church, since he does some of his most deadly work there. In fact, we should actually expect disunity among professing Christians because Satan always has his false-teachers and counterfeit Christians in the church. So our job is simply to pursue unity with God because that is when we will also find unity with others who are also becoming one with God.

When Jesus talked about Him being our Shepherd and us being His sheep, He explained that this meant that He is speaking to us and leading us and we are hearing His voice and following Him. But He also explained that this meant that we can come to know Him: "I know My sheep and My sheep know Me – just as the Father knows Me and I know the Father" (John 10:14). That is mind-boggling that Jesus said He is leading us to know the Father and Jesus the same way that They know one another. Obviously we all have a long way to go, but this is the goal Jesus is leading us toward – that we would truly come to know the Father and Jesus (and the Spirit also). Maybe that is why Jesus said, "I have come that they may have life, and have it to the full" (John 10:10) – by leading us to know the Father and the Son.

Paul lived for that passion of knowing the Father and Jesus. Before he met Jesus, his passion was self-achievement by seeking to please God by his own works, righteousness and dedication. But once he met Jesus, all that he had lived for earlier became so much rubbish compared to "the surpassing greatness of <u>knowing</u> Christ Jesus my Lord, for whose sake I have lost all things. I consider them rubbish, that I may gain Christ and be found in Him, not having a righteousness of my own that comes from the law, but that which is through faith in Christ – the righteousness that comes from God and is by faith. I want to <u>know</u> Christ and the power of His resurrection and the fellowship of sharing in His sufferings, becoming like Him in His death, and so, somehow, to attain to [the power of] the resurrection from the dead [which is LIFE]" (Philippians 3:7-11).

Peter lived for that same passion too. Earlier in his time with Jesus, Peter kept insisting that things should be done his way (such as Matthew 16:21-23; 26:31-35 with 26:69-75; Galatians 2:11-16). But as he matured in Jesus, he finally came to understand that "God's divine power has given us everything we need for life and godliness <u>through our knowledge of Him</u> who called us by His own glory and goodness. Through these He has given us His very great and precious promises, so that through them you may participate in the divine nature and escape the corruption in the world caused by evil desires" (2 Peter 1:3-4). He went on to talk about how we should make every effort to add to our faith goodness, knowledge, self-control, perseverance, godliness, brotherly kindness and love. For if we possess these things in increasing measure, they will "keep us from being ineffective and unproductive <u>in our knowledge of our Lord Jesus Christ</u>" (verses 5-8). And then Peter said, "For if you do these things, you will never fall, and you will receive a rich welcome into the eternal kingdom of our Lord and Savior Jesus Christ" (verses 10-11).

The author of Hebrews understood that same passion too. He quoted the prophecy that God gave to Jeremiah about what this new covenant would be like that Jesus came to bring us through His death on the cross (Jeremiah 31:31-34). He said there would be four qualities of this new covenant: 1) God will put His laws in our minds and write them on our hearts, 2) God will be our God, and we will be His people, 3) we will no longer have to teach our neighbor or brother to know the Lord "because <u>they will all know Him</u>, from the least of them to the greatest," and 4) God will forgive our wickedness and will remember our sins no more"

(Hebrews 8:10-12). That third truth means there are no longer a limited group of believers who are assigned to know God and to try to teach others to know Him too (such as priests and Levites under old covenant), but now all believers from the least of them to the greatest will know the Lord – because we all have the Holy Spirit living in us leading us to know Jesus and the Father as They lead us into LIFE!!

This helps us to understand that the essence of the life that Jesus came to give us is first and foremost a spiritual life where we come back into this right relationship with God again. Here we come to know God as our Father, Jesus as our Lord and Husband, and the Holy Spirit as our Teacher/Coach/Counselor. Here we come to know God in all the glory and fullness of His grace and truth (John 1:14-18). Here we see the glory of the Lord with an unveiled face, where God makes His light to shine in our hearts to give us the light of the <u>knowledge</u> of the glory of God in the face of Christ" (2 Corinthians 3:18; 4:6). Now obviously we all have a long way to go. We only see through a mirror dimly, and we only know in part. But someday when we are finally with the Lord, we will see Him face to face and then we shall <u>know</u> fully even as we are fully known (1 Corinthians 13:9-12).

This is the life that Jesus wants to give us right now during our time on earth – a spiritual life where we can know the Father and His Son Jesus through the work of the Holy Spirit living inside of us. And for those who get a taste of this life, this spiritual life becomes the passion of our lives. Like Paul we will forget what is behind and strain toward what is ahead and press on toward the goal to win the prize for which God has called us heavenward in Christ Jesus (Philippians 3:13-14). And I believe that this is simply the reality of the LIFE Jesus came to bring us, "Now this is eternal life: that they may know You, the only true God, and Jesus Christ, Whom You have sent" (John 17:3). And that is what the ultimate glory of heaven will be – the eternal life of perfectly knowing God as Father, Jesus as Husband, and the Spirit as the Living Water satisfying our deepest longings for all of eternity (Revelation 21-22).

Now someday in the future Jesus will also give us the perfect physical life we so long for as well – in the redemption of the resurrected body (Romans 8:18-25) and the ultimate new heaven and new earth where all death is forever destroyed from God's kingdom (Revelation 21-22). Jesus came to deliver us from every form of death, spiritual as well as physical, temporal as well as eternal. From our perspective, we want God to intervene now to give us physical health and pleasure and life to the full. But from God's perspective, God knows that the spiritual life is infinitely more important. So that is where He has chosen to work first. And He invites us to trust His decision and join Him in that passion to find and live spiritual life to the full now first and foremost as the passion of our lives.

Now when we do grow in spiritual life, we will find that this has a huge impact in our physical lives as well. Sin always leads to death while righteousness always leads to life. So the more we love and obey God and do things God's way in our spiritual life, the more we will be able to enjoy our physical life and pleasures in the way God designed (1 Timothy 4:1-5). In fact, it is actually lies of Satan that try to keep us from enjoying the things that God has created for us to enjoy, especially family and food (no wonder there is so much confusion in our world today about marriage, sex, family, food, and drink). God actually wants to help us enjoy these things the way He designed them to be enjoyed. Then we can enjoy them fully and give God thanks, as we enjoy them according to the Word of God and prayer.

Of course, we still live in a fallen world under the curse. So there is still a lot of pain and suffering. But even though we suffer in this cursed world where we live, we are able to rest in God's love and presence with us, knowing that "our present suffering is not worth comparing with the glory that will be revealed in us" (Romans 8:18-39). So we can endure the pain in the anticipation of the day when we will receive the redemption of our bodies and we will live in glorified bodies enjoying physical and spiritual pleasures forever (Psalm 16:11; Revelation 21-22). And it is so exciting to know that even in the physical suffering of life God works all these things together for good, especially for the good of conforming us more and more to the likeness of His Son Jesus (Romans 8:28-29). I am sure we all have seen so many times how God is able to take the suffering of life and deepen us so much in our relationship and love with God. It is often in the deepest valleys of life where we come to know God in a more personal and real way as we experience His love and feel Him carrying us through. It's not that we love the pain, but we love the gain.

One of the big lessons I have learned is that God wants me seeking first His kingdom and His righteousness. Rather than worrying about the physical things of this life and living to lay up treasures on this earth, God invites me to live my life first and foremost for Him (Matthew 6:19-34). Jesus promised that when we do seek first the kingdom of God and His righteousness, all these other things of this life will be added to us as well (maybe in this lifetime and definitely in the life to come). Now we do still live on this planet, and we are still responsible to work hard and provide for ourselves and our families (Ephesians 4:28; 6:5-9; 1 Timothy 5:8). But we are called to live so that everything we do, even at our jobs, is ultimately unto the Lord and for His glory and for His kingdom (1 Corinthians 10:31-33; Colossians 3:22-25). We are called to live as citizens of heaven, who set our minds and hearts on things above where we now live with the Father, Jesus, and the Spirit in their kingdom (Philippians 3:20-21; Colossians 3:1-4). That is when we will come to know God as He really is. And the more we come to know Him, the more we will find and live life to the full.

So God invites us to trust Him to know what He is doing. He wants to lead us into the fullness of spiritual life first, a life where we learn again to know God as Father, Jesus as Husband, and the Spirit as Teacher, a life where we come home and learn to live as God's family again resting in His love and growing in His grace. He also wants to help us enjoy our physical life as much as possible by teaching us how to enjoy it more and more the way He designed it to be enjoyed. But we accept that we live in a sinful, cursed world and we live in bodies that are aging and dying. So we wait patiently but eagerly for that day of the resurrection when our bodies will be redeemed and death will be forever destroyed. That is when we will have new bodies to enjoy a new heaven and a new earth where we will live a perfect spiritual life and a perfect physical life in incomprehensible pleasures forever. That is when we will enjoy fully what David wrote, "You have made known to me the path of life; You will fill me with joy in Your presence, with eternal pleasure at Your right hand" (Psalm 16:11). That is why we should be passionate about knowing God our Father, Jesus our Husband, and the Holy Spirit our Teacher more and more every day. That is what life is all about. That is real living. That is the life that Jesus came to bring us now in this lifetime. That is a taste of heaven we enjoy here on earth. And it is that taste that will keep us pressing on for the day when we will enjoy the full banquet in heaven of life to the full forever!!

"Now this is eternal life: that they may know You, the only true God, and Jesus Christ Whom You have sent." LET'S LIVE!!!

Conclusion

Life in the Eye of the Needle

I remember vividly being at a pastors' meeting where men were sharing their testimonies about how God had saved them from lives of terrible sin and the devastation it brings. And I sat there feeling like I did not have any testimony I could share. After all, I had accepted Jesus as my Lord and Savior when I was seven, I felt called to the ministry at age eight, and I grew up serving the Lord and achieving "righteousness" as defined by the church at that time. It wasn't until later that day when I had some time alone with my Lord that He reminded me of His encounter with the rich young ruler (Matthew 19:16-30). And it finally dawned on me that for those of us who are "rich" in our self-righteousness of the law, it may actually be a greater miracle when we finally realize how "wretched, pitiful, poor, blind and naked" we really are and we finally repent and let Jesus come in (Revelation 3:14-22). I knew I was not "rich" in money, but I was rich in self-righteousness, in godly heritage, in educational achievements, in hard work, in ministry accomplishments. Like Paul I had great reasons for being confident in myself and my abilities to please and impress God (Philippians 3:4-6).

As I thought then about what Jesus said about how hard it is for a "rich" man to enter into the kingdom of heaven, I realized that maybe it is easier for terrible sinners to repent because they know they are sinners and they know the terrible consequences of sin. But for those of us who are truly rich in our self-righteousness and spiritual achievements, it takes a miracle of God for us finally to admit we are messed-up sinners just like everyone else. That's why Jesus said that it is hard for a rich man to enter the kingdom of heaven. In fact, He said it is easier for a camel to go through the eye of a needle than for a rich man to enter the kingdom of God (whether Jesus was referring to a "needle gate" into Jerusalem where camels would have to get down on their knees or to an actual sewing needle, either was almost or totally impossible). And when the disciples asked, "Who then can be saved," Jesus said something that excited me so much, "With man this is impossible, but with God all things are possible." So maybe I actually had a greater testimony to share because God had done something that was humanly impossible – God had humbled a self-righteous person like me and brought me to Jesus and to the true righteousness which only He can produce.

Since then as I have looked back over all the things that the Lord has taught me and all the ways He has changed me, I have seen them as experiences I have had "in the eye of the needle." And I have marveled at all the things the Lord has done to break me, humble me, convict me, reprogram me, and totally change the ways I think and act and live and minister. And I stand amazed at this outpouring of grace to a "chief of sinners" like me that He would have mercy on me and pour out His grace on me so abundantly (just as He did on Paul – 1 Timothy 1:12-17).

So what I have shared in the preceding chapters are simply lessons learned in the eye of the needle. And though there might have been times that I thought that I might deserve even 1% credit for these things, now I realize that 100% of the credit goes to Jesus. And that means 0% of the credit belongs to me. I am a miracle of God's grace that shows that what is totally impossible with men it totally possible with God. God makes the impossible possible. And He has in my life.

The exciting thing that Jesus went on to tell His disciples is that when we are willing to leave everything to follow Him, that is when we will receive a hundred times as much in this lifetime of anything we have lost – and then someday we will inherit eternal life as well (with eternal riches and rewards too). I would suggest this is talking primarily about what we find in Jesus and His spiritual kingdom because that is so much greater than all the riches of this world (we shouldn't expect or want 100 wives if we lose one). It's like what Paul said, "I consider everything a loss compared to the surpassing greatness of knowing Christ Jesus my Lord, for whose sake I have lost all things. I consider them rubbish, that I may gain Christ and be found in Him, not having a righteousness of my own that comes from the law, but that which is through faith in Christ – the righteousness that comes from God and is by faith. I want to know Him and the power of His resurrection and the fellowship of sharing in His suffering, becoming like Him in His death, and so, somehow, to attain to the resurrection from the dead" (Philippians 3:4-11).

At this time in my spiritual journey, I realize more than ever that I have not arrived. I am still pressing on to take hold of everything that Jesus has provided for me in His death, resurrection, and exaltation. The Lord is tantalizing me with the intriguing possibility that I have spent too much of my life in the shadows of the works of law in the energy of flesh and that there is an exciting new creation out there for me to explore and enjoy filled with all the riches of God's grace that are mine for the enjoying by faith as I dare to live in the Spirit as He fills me and leads me into all that Jesus has for me. So forgetting what is behind and straining toward what is ahead, I press on toward the goal to win the prize for which God has called us heavenward in Christ Jesus (Philippians 3:12-15).

So I share these truths that I have learned "in the eye of the needle" through many long years of struggle in the prayer that they can help many more fully "enter into the kingdom of heaven" where we can "get the eternal life" the rich young ruler wanted and that I want and that God wants us to want. God invites us each to come to Jesus and to that pure delight of opening the door and letting Him come in to eat with us and we with Him (Revelation 3:20).

That is when we are no longer making Jesus sick with our lukewarmness where we think we are rich and having acquired wealth and in need of nothing. But instead we have repented and accepted that we are wretched, pitiful, poor, blind and naked. And now we run to Jesus to buy of Him the gold refined in the fire, so we can become rich; and white clothes to wear, so we can cover our shameful nakedness; and salve to put on our eyes, so we can see (Revelation 3:14-22). That is when we will enjoy feasting with Jesus and celebrating together with him just like the prodigal son, rather than slaving away in the field like the older son who was boiling over with resentment and unable to enjoy the party (Luke 15:11-32). That is when we will be loving Jesus and truly believing in Him and will be filled with joy inexpressible and full of glory as we receive the amazing fullness of our spiritual salvation (1 Peter 1:8-9). That is when we are becoming the answer to Jesus' prayer and passion as we are becoming truly one with Him just like He and the Father are one, with Jesus abiding in us and we in Him just as the Father abides in Jesus and Jesus abides in the Father (John 14-17).

My prayer is that the Holy Spirit would use my story and the things the Lord has taught me to help you on your walk with the Lord, so that you too can discover and enjoy more fully that life to the full that Jesus came to bring us (John 10:10). My prayer is that you could find and enjoy it much earlier and more fully than I have ever been able to do. My prayer is simply that you would turn to Jesus and give Him absolute control in your life, so that God can do immeasurably more than all we can ask or imagine, according to the power of Jesus at work within us, so that to God may be all the glory in us as the church and in Christ Jesus in our generation and throughout all the generations for ever and ever (Ephesians 3:20-21).